Moving to the United States of America and Immigration

Mark A Cooper

Copyright © 2008 by Mark A. Cooper

ISBN 0-7414-4625-1

Published by:

INFI∞ITY
PUBLISHING.COM

1094 New DeHaven Street, Suite 100
West Conshohocken, PA 19428-2713
Info@buybooksontheweb.com
www.buybooksontheweb.com
Toll-free (877) BUY BOOK
Local Phone (610) 941-9999
Fax (610) 941-9959

Printed in the United States of America

Printed on Recycled Paper

Published March 2008

Dedicated to Craig, my son

You have no idea how proud of you, I am.

Contents

Foreword

If you are considering making the move to the United States, either on a permanent basis or just to spend a few weeks or months in the United States, then this is the book for you.

Moving to the United States and Buying a Home has been written to help anyone wanting to know what it takes to make the move. Thousands of people make the move each year; many are tourists, immigrants, temporary workers, actors, businessmen and woman, students, retirees and holiday home owners. *(Illegal immigrants are in the millions; however they have broken the laws of the U.S. This book is intended to show you how to do it legally)*

The state changes will only impact on buying a home and not on immigration. Immigration is done on a federal level.

When my wife and I first talked about moving to the United States, we thought it would be just a case of selling our home and making the move. Once we started to investigate further, it did become very daunting. The process can become very stressful, taking a vacation to Disney in Orlando and renting a villa, is a very different thing to making a house purchase or making the move. This book will show you how, explain how to adapt to new customs, traditions, money, banks, schools, education, paying bills, obtaining insurance and even driving in the United States. (The wrong side of the road).

Starting a new life in a new country is an exciting time, if you follow the process and tick off one thing at a time it becomes less stressful. The majority of Americans are 3rd or 4th generation immigrants. Many of their great grandparents where first processed at Ellis Island (The State of Liberty) 25 million people arrived through Ellis Island and the Port of New York between 1892-1924. Today they are able to search the website and download images of the actual immigration forms. So it's nothing new, however by reading this book it will help to reduce stress, save you a lot of time and money.

Buying a home is a complicated process, even in your home country. When you are buying a home in another State or country the complications can seem endless. If you are thinking of buying a home in United States, this book will help you through the process.

If you have spent time in Florida you will quickly see why thousands of people are moving to the Sunshine State. Every month 150 families move to Florida on a permanent basis. Many are American from northern colder states such as New York, New Jersey, many fly down from the windy city Chicago. Thousands have moved south from Canada. Plus many more thousands have flown half way around the world including Great Britain, Italy, Ireland, Poland and Asia.

The Hottest immigration state, Florida

Why Florida? Florida gets 300 days of sunshine per year and has an average temperature of 71 degrees Fahrenheit or (21 degrees Celsius). It has 1500 miles of coast, sea temperatures get up to 90 degrees F. Dolphins swim around the coast, Sea Turtles nest on the beaches. Alligators swim in the rivers, lakes and can be seen basking in the sun on the banks, (Be warned)

The people of Florida are friendly, most have moved from the *rat race* London, New York, Chicago, Detroit and other major busy colder towns and cities from around the world. They arrive to a warm climate, and a slower pace. The abundance of sunshine and proximity to the sea seems to make people smile; you will find yourself talking to strangers as you walk either along the beaches or the streets. The children are free to play almost every day of the year outside of bikes, skateboards, basket ball or other sports and activities.

There is a hell of a lot more to Florida than just Mickey Mouse and having a warm climate, where the local speak English (Although Spanish makes up 16% of the language). It has the World's greatest beaches. If you have been here, you will know what I mean. Plus no income tax.

California

The State offers unparalleled diversity, whether north or south California. The diversity of culture, scenic beauty and things to do make California unlike any other place in the world. The 12 Regions: San Diego, Shasta Cascade, Bay Area, Central Coast, North Coast, Orange County, Los Angeles, Central Valley, Desert, Gold Country, High Sierra and Inland Empire. You can mingle with fashionistas and Celebs on a drive from Newport Beach to Los Angeles.

Whatever of the 50 States you choose; it's not hard to see why over 5 million people per year try to immigrate to the United States, either legally or otherwise. 'The land of opportunity' has proven time and time again, that those who wish to accomplish success; The United States is the greatest place on earth to accomplish your goals. Some of the famous immigrants include Bob Hope, Arnold Schwarzenegger, Placido Domingo, Michael J. Fox, Angela Lansbury, Sidney Poitier, Andre Previn, Oscar de la Renta, Charles Atlas, Irving Berlin, Frank Capra, Al Jolson, Charlie Chaplin, William Shatner, Jerry Springer, Max Factor and Albert Einstein.

Section 1) Visa or Green Card?

The main problem facing people who wish to move to the United States is obtaining a work visa. The United States has enough of its own scroungers, hangers on, those who want the government and tax payers to look after them, pay to educate their children and pay their medical bills. Therefore if you want to move to the United States you will need a visa. You can't just turn up, rent a home and expect to go and find a job. That's what the illegal immigrants do. The United States will allow you to move here, either temporary or full time, it just want you to apply correctly, the same way generations have done. Similarly if you have money, you can't just pick up and move. You have to contribute something to the country.

How do you move? You need a Visa or a Green card.

Millions of foreign visitors travel to the U.S. each year. Others come to live here permanently. International visitors and immigrants add greatly to the nation's cultural, education and economic life. The United States welcomes them. At the same time, they need to do everything we can to keep everyone here, safe. The policy of the United States government is that they believe in secure borders and open doors.

A citizen of a foreign country, wishing to enter the U.S., generally must first obtain a visa, either a nonimmigrant visa for temporary stay, or an immigrant visa for permanent residence. The type of visa you must have is defined by immigration law, and relates to the purpose of your travel.

Most Canadian citizens and many citizens from Visa Waiver Program countries can come to the U.S. without a visa if they meet certain requirements. Visa waiver travelers from ALL 27 Visa Waiver Program countries must present a machine-readable passport at the U.S. port of entry to enter the U.S. without a visa; otherwise a U.S. visa is required.

Nonimmigrant visas are for international travelers, (citizens of other countries), coming to the U.S. temporarily. This visa allows you to travel to a U.S. port-of-entry (airport, for example) and request permission of the Department of Homeland Security immigration inspector to enter the U.S. Be aware a visa does not guarantee entry into the United States. International travelers come to the U.S. for a wide variety of reasons, including tourism, business, medical treatment and certain types of temporary work. The type of visa needed is defined by immigration law, and relates to the principal purpose of your travel. While in the U.S., temporary visitors are restricted to the activity or reason for which their nonimmigrant visa was issued, with few exceptions.

Section 2) Visa Waiver Program.

Overview – what is the Visa Waiver Program?

The Visa Waiver Program (VWP) enables nationals of certain countries to travel to the United States for tourism or business for stays of 90 days or less without obtaining a visa. The program was established in June 1986 with the objective of eliminating unnecessary barriers to travel, thus helping the tourism industry, and permitting the Department of State to focus consular resources in other areas. VWP eligible travelers may apply for a visa, if they prefer to do so. Not all countries participate in the VWP, and not all travelers from VWP countries are eligible to use the program. VWP travelers are screened prior to admission into the United States, and they are enrolled in the Department of Homeland Security US Visit program.

Countries that participate in the Visa Waiver Program (VWP)

27 countries participate in the Visa Waiver Program, as shown below:

Andorra	Iceland	Norway
Australia	Ireland	Portugal
Austria	Italy	San Marino
Belgium	Japan	Singapore
Brunei	Liechtenstein	Slovenia
Denmark	Luxembourg	Spain

Finland	Monaco	Sweden
France	The Netherlands	Switzerland
Germany	New Zealand	United Kingdom

If however you are planning to stay in the United States longer than 90 days, or you wish to work or attend a university for a temporary period, then you will need a visa. In the majority of cases the spouse and children (*Children up to the age of 21*) can qualify for derivative visas based on the visa that you will be travelling on. I would recommend you consult with the American Embassy or consulate for more information about the limitations of such derivate visas. Details for the American embassy and U.S Consulate are in contact details at the back of the book.

The following list gives different types of non-immigrant visas that the United States grants for specific travel purposes. Should your activity not fit the description on the following pages, then you may need to apply for an exchange visitor Visa, known as J-1 or a temporary work visa H-1.

Section 3) The Green Card Lottery.

Every Year, the Diversity Visa Lottery (DV) Program Grants 50,000 visas to people all around the world. All 50,000 Winners are issued a US GREEN CARD authorizing them and their families to live and work in the United States!

This official program will make permanent residence visas available to persons meeting the simple, but strict, eligibility requirements. Applicants for Diversity Visa are chosen by a computer-generated random lottery drawing. The U.S. government makes available 50,000 permanent residence visas each year for this program. Application to this program is open for most individuals worldwide that fulfill the two basic entry requirements. The visas are distributed among six geographic regions with a greater number of visas going to regions with lower rates of immigration, and with no visas going to citizens of countries sending more than 50,000 immigrants to the U.S. in the past five years. Within each region, no one country may receive more than seven percent of the available Diversity Visas in any one year. The Immigrant Diversity Visa Lottery has been established in the 1996 Immigration Act in order to give immigration opportunity to natives from countries other than the main source of immigration to the U.S.A. This official U.S. government program aims to diversify the American population by creating an immigration opportunity to live, work and study in the U.S.A.

Countries that <u>can't</u> participate in the green card lottery:

Anguilla
Bermuda
British Virgin Islands

Caicos Islands
Canada
Cayman Islands
China
Colombia
Dominican Republic
El Salvador
Falkland Islands
Haiti
India
Jamaica
Mexico
Montserrat
Pakistan
Philippines
Pitcairn
South Korea
St. Helena
Turks
United Kingdom
Vietnam

Yes, the United Kingdom, so if you're a Brit, you can't apply.

History of the Green Card Lottery Program

THE DIVERSITY VISA LOTTERY TO WIN GREEN CARDS WAS A PROGRAM BY WHICH A CATEGORY OF IMMIGRANTS FROM UNDERREPRESENTED COUNTRIES AND THOSE ADVERSELY EFFECTED BY THE IMMIGRATION AND NATIONALITY ACT AMENDMENTS OF 1965 (P.L. 89-236) WERE TO RECEIVE A SPECIAL IMMIGRATION BENEFIT. IN 1986 THE UNITED STATES CONGRESS ATTEMPTED TO ASSIST RECENTLY DISADVANTAGED IMMIGRANTS WITH AN EMPHASIS ON PERSONS FROM THE IRISH ISLES OBTAIN SOME SPECIAL WAY TO IMMIGRATE AND RECEIVE A GREEN CARD TO THE UNITED STATES. THE SPONSORS OF THE LEGISLATION, (AMONG THEM PROMINENT IRISH-AMERICAN MEMBERS OF CONGRESS) DEVISED A LOTTERY

PROGRAM THAT WOULD GRANT GREEN CARDS TO PERSONS FROM OTHERWISE UNDERREPRESENTED COUNTRIES. SINCE THAT INITIAL PROGRAM, CHANGES HAVE BEEN MADE. THE CONGRESSIONALLY MANDATED DIVERSITY IMMIGRANT VISA PROGRAM IS ALSO KNOWN AS THE DIVERSITY LOTTERY PROGRAM OR THE GREEN CARD LOTTERY. IT IS ADMINISTERED ON AN ANNUAL BASIS BY THE U.S. DEPARTMENT OF STATE AND CONDUCTED UNDER THE TERMS OF SECTION 203© OF THE IMMIGRATION AND NATIONALITY ACT (INA). SECTION 131 OF THE IMMIGRATION ACT OF 1990 (PUB. L. 101-649) AMENDED INA 203 TO PROVIDE FOR A NEW CLASS OF IMMIGRANTS KNOWN AS "DIVERSITY IMMIGRANTS" (DV IMMIGRANTS).

Section 4) If You Have Family in the US or Immediate Relatives.

Quotas & Categories:

The total quota for all preference categories is currently 725,000 per year. The US immigration year runs from 1st October – 30th September. These numbers are further divided into more categories.

Relatives of United States citizens and of Permanent resident aliens (Green card holders) are limited to 500,000 a year. Immediate relatives are also included in this number, although there is NO limit on the number of visas that are issued to immediate relatives. An immediate relative is a spouse and unmarried children under the age of 21. Step parents and step children are included if the marriage took place before the child became 18, and foreign children if adopted before age 16.

1st Preference. 25,000 Unmarried children of United States citizens, plus their children.

2nd Preference. 115,000 Spouses and children of green card holders. Normally at least 60% of these go to spouses and children. The remainders go to unmarried sons & daughters.

3rd preference. 25,000 married children of any age of United States citizens and their spouses and children.

4th Preference. 65,000 brothers and sisters of Unites States citizens and their spouses, plus children. As long as the United States citizen is over 21.

11

However if you have no family in the United States, then you have you use another route. There are many ways to apply for a visa; I have shown every way possible in current legislation.

Section 5) Academics and Researchers.

Students: If you want to study at a University (academic institution) in the United States you can apply for a student Visa. Known as an F-1 visa. If however you are a student on a full course of study at an academic institution outside the United States and are required to study at a U.S academic institution for a term as part of your curriculum, you can apply for an exchange visitor Visa. Known as a J-1 visa.

Lecturer or Professor. As a member of the academic profession, you can come to the United States to engage in usual academic activities. You can travel on a B-1 visa, provided there is no remuneration from a source within the United States. (Other than expenses for the incidental visit) You are not allowed to work at any time on this visa.

Medical Practitioner. If you are training, and this involves practical experience and instruction in the various disciplines of medicine under the supervision and direction of faculty physicians at the US medical schools hospital, then you can apply for the B-1 visa. Provided that the post is an approved part of your schools education and you do not get paid by the hospital. You will first have to obtain a letter from the US medical school outlining the nature and the duration of the visa and the source of remuneration, if any. This will all have to be processed together with your application.

Section 6) O-Visa's.

Actors, Athletes, Sports men/woman and Entertainers.

If you are one of the above (The David Beckham's, Elton John's and Catherine Zeta-Jones's) and wish to travel to the United States, you must obtain a sponsor, He/she or company must file an application on form I-129 O or P. This must be applied for with BCIS. Bureau of Citizenship and Immigration Services (BCIS)

The list below is the type of Visas that might be granted in this type of case, but it's your sponsor or employer who must contact the BCIS for application information.

O-1 Visa: Are for people extraordinary ability in the fields of science, art, education, business and athletics, and workers in film and TV whose work has earned them either national or international achievement. You and your support personnel (Victoria Beckham's, hairdresser) may be able to enter the USA on an O visa. The O-2 Visa is for those who are part of an athlete's or entertainer's performance and have experience and skills that are not available in the US location of the event. You may be able to apply for an O-2 Visa to accompany the O-1 Visa holder. This is a grey area, as the US has for example hairdressers and trainers for athletes, but one can argue that a certain hairdresser knows to get a type of style or trainer knows how far to push an athlete he has been working with.

Section 7) P-Visa's.

P-1 Visa: An artist or entertainer plus essential support personnel may be liable to enter the United States on this Visa. However individual members of the entertainment industry are not eligible. But individual athletes are allowed to apply. For those members of the entertainment industry, the visa will be issued for a specific event only, such as a football match (Soccer) or world/Olympic games etc. Those individual athletes may be admitted for 5 years and a team for 6 months.

P-2 Visa: As an Athlete or entertainer, either an individual or group, involved in a reciprocal exchange program between an organization in the United States and one or more foreign countries that provides for the temporary exchange of entertainers and artists, you may be able to enter the United States on the P-2 Visa.

P-3 Visa: If you are an artist or entertainer, either an individual or group, who wants to perform, teach or even coach under a program that is unique, you can apply for the P-3 Visa.

P-4 Visa: These are granted to the spouse and unmarried children under 21 of people granted either P-1, P-2 or P-3 Visas, although they are permitted to study. I feel that the qualifications are not as stringent as for O visas. However there is an overlap between the uses and qualifications needed to apply for both O and P visas.

Cultural Exchange Visitors, *See Category Q- Visas.*

If you are participating in an international cultural exchange program designed to provide on the job training, employment and the sharing of your native culture, you will need to apply for a classification Q visa. The Activity in question has to be approved in advance by the Bureau of Citizenship and Immigration Services (BCIS) in the United States on the basis of an application, Form 1-129Q. Must be filed by your United States sponsor.

Section 8) Q-Visa's.

A Q Visa application is approved for the length of the program or for a maximum of 15 months, whatever is the shorter. A Q visa holder who has spent 15 months in the United States may not be issued a visa or be readmitted under the Q visa classification unless you have resided and been physically present outside the United States for at least 12 months.

Requirements for Q Visa

The culture sharing must take place in a school, business, museum or a place where the public is exposed to aspects of a foreign culture as part of a structured program. The Cultural component has to be an integral part of the applicant's employment and training, and must be designed to exhibit the attitude, customs, heritage, history and traditions of the country of nationality. The sponsoring organization must demonstrate that is has the ability to conduct a responsible international cultural exchange program and also that it has the financial ability to remunerate the applicant and offer the applicant a wage and full working conditions comparable to those in line with local state and county employment laws. Plus the applicant must be at least 18 and qualified to perform the stated service of labor or receive the specified type of training, and have the ability to communicate regarding his or her culture. There is NO provision for the issue of visas to the spouse and unmarried children under 21.

Section 9) R-Visa's.

Religious Workers.

A Minister or religious worker can apply for the Religious worker classification R-Visa, if for two years immediately preceding the time of application; you have to be a member of a religious denomination that has a genuine non-profit religious organization in the United States. The term religious workers include counselors, social workers, health care, missionaries, and workers for religious hospitals, translators and religious broadcasters.

The initial admission period for ministers and religious workers under R-Visa is three years. However an employer can file a form I-129 application with the BCIS to request an extension. This extension will not be granted for more than a TOTAL of 5 years. When you apply for your visa as a voluntary worker, you should also include a letter from your United States employer containing detailed information as the intended nature of your trip, along with foreign permanent residence address, the name and address of your initial destination in the United States and the anticipated duration of your stay.

Examples include nuns, monks, and religious brothers and sisters. A religious occupation means a habitual engagement in an activity which relates to a traditional religious function. Examples include liturgical workers, religious instructors or cantors, catechists, workers in religious hospitals, missionaries, religious translators, or religious broadcasters. It does not however include janitors, maintenance workers, clerks, fund raisers, or similar occupations.

Spouses and children may accompany or follow to join the visa holder on R-2 status.

Essential documentation needed to bring to the consulate if first applying for an R-1 visa or to attach to Form I-129, Petition for a Nonimmigrant Worker.

1) A letter from the authorizing officials of the religious organization establishing that the proposed services and the alien qualify.

2) A letter or letters from the authorizing officials of the religious denomination or organization attesting to the alien's membership in the religious denomination explaining, in detail, the alien's religious work and all employment during the past two years and the proposed temporary employment.

3) A copy of the tax-exempt certificate showing the religious organization and any affiliate which will employ the alien, is a bona fide organization in the U.S. and is exempt from taxation in accordance with Section 501(c)(3) of the Internal Revenue Code of 1986.

4) Copy of membership certificate/documentation establishing the relationship between the U.S. religious organization and the organization abroad of which the alien was a member.

5) One recent photograph 1 & 1/2 inches square (37mm x 37mm) of each applicant, with the entire face visible. The picture should be taken before a light background and without head covering.

6) A passport, valid for travel to the United States for at least six months longer than your intended visit.

Section 10) I-Visa's.

Media workers.

If you are a representative of a foreign media travelling to the United States on a case or assignment, you may be eligible for classification under the I-Visa category. This includes members of the press, TV, Radio, Film and now Internet news whose activities are essential to the foreign media function such as reporters, film crew, and editors. ONLY those who are actually involved in the news-gathering process are eligible. The Immigration and Nationality Act is very specific about the qualification requirements for the I-Visa. These visas will only be granted to members of the media and freelance journalists and employees of independent production companies under contract to media organizations. Members of the media engaged in the production or distribution of film will only qualify for I-Visas if the material being filmed will be used for news and the primary point of distribution is outside the United States. I-Visas include the spouses and unmarried children under the age of 21. Plus they are also appropriate for foreign journalists working for an overseas office of a United States Network or other new media. If that said journalist is reporting on US events for an American audience, them an H or O visa will be required.

Section 11) K-Visa's.

Fiancé (e) s

The K-1 Visa is required if you are planning to marry a United States citizen. You can use the K-Visa to enter the United States providing you are going to get married in 90 days of entry, including any unmarried children under the age of 21. (The children apply for a K-2 Visa and the dog a K-9 Visa). *The K-9 visa was a joke, but later you will read how to bring your pets to the United States.*

A K-1 Visa holder can apply to work immediately upon arrival. Once married he/she can apply for a green card. If the marriage does not take place in the 90 days, then he/she must leave the country, the K-1 Visa can **NOT** be extended. It takes approx 3-5 months to apply and receive your K-1 Visa to enter the United States. Many couples simply marry each other, either abroad or in the United States and then apply direct for a green card. Please note it is illegal to enter the United States of America as a visitor with the intentions of getting married. As you can guess it's also illegal to get married just to remain in the country and apply for a green card. There are stringent checks, to stop marriages of convenience. The immigration department will come unannounced and check you and your home, your bed and where you're clean and dirty laundry is being kept. They are experts at this and are not fooled. You must not leave the United States before receiving your green card without permission from the INS. Note you can not apply for a K-Visa to marry a non United States citizen, such as a green card holder. However if the green card holder becomes a citizen then you can. *See Green Cards.*

Section 12) Foreign Government Representatives, Employees of International Organizations and NATO. G-Visa's.

To qualify for a G-1 Visa, one must be entering the United States on official duties. The G-1 Visa is for representatives of a foreign government who are living and working in the United States, plus staff. The G-2 Visa is for representatives of a foreign government who are travelling to the United States on a temporary basis. The G-2 Visa is normally used for those attending meetings etc. Representatives of non-recognized or non-member governments are eligible for G-3 and G-4 Visa's.

NATO representatives have various classifications. If you are seeking admission to the United States under provision of the agreement on the North Atlantic Treaty Organization, national representatives and international staff. The classifications are NATO-1, NATO-2, NATO-3, NATO-4, and NATO-5. Armed forces personnel are exempt from passport and visa requirements if they are attached to NATO allied Head quarters in the United States. They must however carry Military ID cards and NATO travel orders.

With the exception of a head of a state or government, who qualify or an A-1 Visa, regardless of the purpose of the visit. The type of visa required by a diplomat depends on the reason for entering the United States. To get an A-1 or A-2 Visa you must be travelling to the United States on behalf of your government, and the purpose of the visit is solely for official activities. Local government officials representing their states, Town, City or Provence do not qualify for the A-Visa. They would need to apply for a B-1 or B-2 Visa. Government officials travelling to the United States to perform non-governmental duties or of a commercial nature, or even as a tourist will require the appropriate H, L or B Visa.

If you are not in any of the groups above, then we move onto the next stage and the more common sourced visas. The next few pages we cover the most common visa (Apart from the tourist visa) plus an in-depth ways on how to apply and make sure your application is successful.

Section 13) H-Visa's.

To work in the United States you must first apply and be accepted for a category H-Visa. These can be valid with extensions for up to 6 years. They are normally granted when you have been offered a form of employment by an American employer. The type of employment must first be approved in advance by the INS. This is done by the employer filing a petition form I-129H or I-129L. In total there are 5 categories of the H-Visa.

H-1B: workers in skilled occupations.

H-1C: Registered nurses.

H-2B: Skilled and unskilled workers.

H-3: Trainees.

H-4: Immediate families of H-1, H-2 and H-3 visa holders.

The procedure for H-Visa application is very complex and subject to change. I would strongly recommend that you seek the services of an experienced immigration lawyer. This will save you time, disappointment and in the long run, money.

Petitions for H-Visa's

In order to be considered as a nonimmigrant under the above classifications the applicant's prospective employer or agent must file Form I-129, Petition for Nonimmigrant Worker, with the United States Citizenship and Immigration Services in the Department of Homeland Security (USCIS). Important Note: It is very important for prospective employers to file the petition as soon as possible (but not more than 6 months before the proposed employment will begin) to provide adequate time for petition and subsequent visa processing.

If we start with the H-1B Visa, 65,000 are issued each year.

The H1-B visa holder can apply for a Green Card if a company wants to sponsor his/her application. These are issued to workers in specialized occupations. Such as Lawyers, Doctors, Accountants, Vets, Nurses, Teachers, Professors and Scientists. Plus hold a degree or equivalent experience. You should also be going to The United States to perform services in a prearranged job.

You may still apply if you do not hold a degree, or three years or more experience. Although your application will be subject to greater scrutiny and thus could be more difficult to obtain.

The 305 foot Statue of Liberty, a long time symbol of Immigration to the United States of America. It was made

and given to America by the French in 1885. It was completed in France a year earlier and was transported in over 200 crates on the French Frigate "Isere" One of its designers was Gustave Eiffel. He also designed a tower you may have heard of in Paris, France. Circa 1903

The position applied for must require a university graduate (it is not possible for an employer to employ a professional person to fill a non-professional/ non-graduate position, example: A doctor can't get a job at MacDonald's, flipping burgers) and the applicant should have all the appropriate background for the position. *Work experience may satisfy this prerequisite if the work was in a field that generally requires a bachelor's degree. Additionally, the foreign worker must be employed in a "professional capacity." This means that the employment must be a legitimate professional job requiring a professional education and paying a commensurate salary. The foreign worker cannot simply be engaged in the employment as a hobby or for religious purposes.*

United States Citizenship and Immigration Services in the Department of Homeland Security (USCIS).

The majority of professions in the United States are controlled and licensed by the local State. This results in over 50 different licensing procedures for every profession. You should first check to see if you can meet the requirements necessary to take the licensing examination. Plus take the exam in the state that you are planning to work in. Your employer must file a labor condition attestation with the department of labor. Before the employer can sponsor someone for an H-1B Visa. They should also prepare the Labor Condition Attestation the prevailing wage for that said position locally. The wage amount must come from the Department of Labor. The wage the employer offers must NOT be less than the prevailing wage determination. To determine this amount the employer and ONLY the employer must register the business with the department of labor. On the next page is a simple step by step guide on how THE EMPLOYER completes the registration process. Please note, I can't stress enough, this MUST be done on the employers computer and not the candidates.

Here is a step-by-step guideline for employers to complete the registration process:

1.   Go to: www.census.gov/epcd/www/naics.html

2.   Enter a keyword that best describes your company's primary business activity in the "NAICS Search" box.   Then make a note of the NAICS Code that best matches your business. It is VITAL that you choose the code that is closest to your actual primary business activity ... otherwise the application could run into problems later. If you are unsure, please contact our office.

3.   Go to: www.plc.doleta.gov/eta_start.cfm

4.   Click "OK" when the auto message appears

5.   Click the blue box marked "Register"

6.   Click the light blue box marked "Setup Employer Profile"

7.   Click the blue box marked "Accept"

8.   Add employer's personal info in the first section marked 'User Profile' — note that it is not necessary to 'tab' through the phone/fax number fields — you will automatically move between the fields as the required number of digits have been entered.

9.   Add the business info in the second section marked "Employer Business Information". Once again, it is not necessary to 'tab' through the E.I.N. number fields. In this section it is necessary to select the NAICS Code that you established in step 2 above.

10.   Add your contact info in the third section marked "Employer Contact Information".

11.   Check that the 'NAICS Code' in section 2 still shows your desired choice and then click on "SUBMIT".

12.   If you get a red (incorrect) error message stating that you entered a 'future date' under 'Year Commenced Business', enter '1111'. This will be accepted and will allow you to register. There will be an opportunity to correct the information once registration is complete.

13.   Once submitted, you will receive an e-mail within 5 business days with a temporary password and instructions on how to finalize the registration process.

Once you have successfully registered on-line, you should receive two e-mails from the U.S. Dept of Labor – one with your Password and another with your PIN. The Password allows you to log in and use your on-line account. The PIN is only used when submitting applications.

Due to the amount of applicants for H1-B Visa's in the IT industry, the government increased the annual quota from 115,000 to 195,000 in 2000 and in 2004 increased it to 215,000. The H-1B Visa are issued for up to three years, although certain countries citizens are given a shorter period. Typically from 1 month to two years. Extensions are common place and normally granted up to a maximum of six years. The H-1A or H-1B Visa holders can apply for permanent residency.

The H-1C Visa was introduced in the fall of 2000 for nurses who wanted to come to the United States to work in certain positions, due to a shortage of health care workers. Only 1000 are issued and they are available for three years and not viable for extension applications. Similarly the H-2B Visa's are for temporary workers also filling in positions for the work shortage, some of these are also for seasonal workers. In the case of the H-2B visa no educational requirements are needed. Experience and qualifications depend on the position applied for. The H-2B visa is temporary and is typically a skilled engineer employed by foreign company and coming to the United Sates to install equipment and train staff.

The H-2B visa has an annual quota of 65,000 and issued for 12 months, although an extension of up to two years can be applied for. The petition for the visa must be applied for by the employer who must also apply for labor certification as above. The processing time for an H-2B visa is normally longer than the processing time for the H-1B visa, by 3-5 months. Once you have spent 3 years in the United States on an H-2B visa you can not apply for another H-2B Visa you have to wait for a 12 month period to elapse.

The H-3 Visa was introduced for trainees coming to the United States for work experience and training in a certain field. The US employer has to provide the INS with statements describing the training offered and the position for which the trainee is going to be trained. It must also explain why the training can't take place in the applicants own country of residence. The training can't be used to provide productive employment. The visa is issued for a maximum of 18 months. Extensions can be applied for but only in certain circumstances, this is because the training is normally completed in 18 months.

H-4 Visas are for spouses and unmarried children under 21 of all the above H-visa holders, However they are NOT permitted to work.

Limit of H1B visa.

Total stay is limited to 6 years. Initial approval is for 3 years, which can be extended for increment of up to 3 years.

✓ **H1B- Re-Stamping?**

A new stamping can be done in any other country at any American consulate, based on the H1B extension approval.

✓ **Multiple Employers?**

H-1B aliens may work for more than one U.S. employer, but must have a Form I-129 petition approved by each employer.

✓ **Travel?**

H1B visa can be multiple entry visas, which allows a person to travel in and out of USA for any number of times, within the specified visa validity.

✓ **Work?**

H-1B aliens may only work for the petitioning U.S. employer, and employer may place the H-1B worker on the work site of another employer.

✓ **Vacation?**

An H-1B alien may be on vacation, sick/ maternity/paternity on strike. As long as alien is associated with the employer.

✓ **Family Status?**

The spouse and unmarried children (under the age of 21) of H1B professionals are allowed to stay in the United States under the H4 category for the same duration as the H1B status.

✓ **Permanent Residency (Green Card)?**

An H1B holder is eligible to seek, permanent residency to USA.

✓ **Changing Employer?**

H1B can be transferred, to a new Employer.

You can also start working for new Employer upon the receipt of H1 transfer case.

✓ **Buying Property?**

H1B holder can buy or sell real estate or any other property in USA.

You can buy lottery or win lottery.

Section 14) E1 Visa's (Treaty Visas).

Over the years the United States has signed treaties with most of the other countries in the world, in particular treaties of 'Friendship, Commerce and Navigation'. These treaties are designed to promote trade and investment between the USA and the other contracting state, thereby encouraging good relations and peace. More recently the USA has entered into a number of Bilateral Investment Treaties with mainly former communist states, designed to promote investment but not generally conferring any trade-related immigration privileges.

Nationals (individuals or companies) of countries with such Treaties with the United States can obtain visas to work in the USA in order to develop and direct their investment in and/or trade with the USA. Such visas are called E-visas, and come in two types:

E-1 Visa Countries

Argentina	China (ROC)	France	Italy	Netherlands	Sweden
Australia	Colombia	Germany	Japan	Norway	Switzerland
Austria	Costa Rica	Greece	Korea	Oman	Thailand
Belgium	Denmark	Honduras	Latvia	Pakistan	Togo
Bolivia	Estonia	Iran	Liberia	Philippines	Turkey
Brunei	Ethiopia	Ireland	Luxembourg	Spain	U.K.
Canada	Finland	Israel	Mexico	Suriname	Yugoslavia

E-2 Visa Countries

Argentina	China (ROC)	Georgia	Kyrgyzstan	Pakistan	Switzerland
Armenia	Colombia	Germany	Latvia	Panama	Thailand
Australia	Congo	Grenada	Liberia	Philippines	Togo
Austria	Costa Rica	Honduras	Luxembourg	Poland	Trinidad and Tobago
Bangladesh	The Czech Republic	Iran	Mexico	Romania	Tunisia
Belarus	Ecuador	Ireland	Morocco	Senegal	Turkey
Belgium	Egypt	Italy	Moldovia	The Slovak Republic	The Ukraine
Bosnia-Herzegovina	Estonia	Jamaica	Mongolia	Spain	United Kingdom
Bulgaria	Ethiopia	Japan	Netherlands	Sri Lanka	Uzbekistan
Cameroon	Finland	Kazakhstan	Norway	Suriname	Yugoslavia
Canada	France	Korea	Oman	Sweden	

The E-Visa is the most common visa, if you wish to move to the United States and you do not have a degree or a sponsor then the E-Visa is for you.

E-1 Visa

There are NO quota restrictions on the E-1 Visa. Spouses of E-1 Visa holders are eligible to work in the United States. The visa is issued for 2 years and can be extended as many times as applied for. So long as you have been a good boy or girl. If you have committed a crime your application may be turned down, this includes members of your family.

Advantages of the E- Visa Classification

- Application for an E-1 Visa is made directly to a U.S. consulate. There is no need to submit a preliminary petition with U.S. Citizenship and Immigration Services (CIS).
- There is no cap on E-1 Visa extensions.

Disadvantages of the E-1 Visa Classification

- E-1 Visa Treaty Traders may only engage in employment that is consistent with the terms and conditions of the activities forming the basis for their E-1 Visa status.
- There are strict requirements on the nationality of individuals and the level of trade necessary to qualify for E-1 Visa status.
- Under NAFTA arrangements, the usual documentary waiver provisions (such as the visa exemption) that normally apply to Canadians do not apply to the E-1 Visa classification.

Family

- Spouses and children under 21 may also receive E-1 Visa status.
- The nationality of a spouse or child of an E-1 Visa treaty trader is not material in determining eligibility for E-1 visa status.
- Spouses may obtain employment authorization.
- Spouses and minor children can also attend school.
- Regulations require only that E-1 Visa visitors intend to depart when their status terminates. E-1 Visa visitors do

not have to maintain a foreign residence that they have no intention of abandoning.

•   Dual Intent: An application for initial admission, change of status, or extension of stay in E-1 Visa classification may not be denied solely on the basis of an approved request for permanent labor certification or a filed or approved immigrant visa preference petition.

•   Individuals may change to E-1 Visa status or extend their E-1 Visa status by filing the necessary documents with the appropriate U.S. Citizenship and Immigration Services (CIS) Service Center. However, most U.S. consuls will adjudicate the E-1 visa application without regard to CIS approval. The consular officers are much more familiar with the E-1 visa category. Therefore, the value of going through the CIS Service Center is debatable.

•   An interesting and little known feature of the E Visa category is that an individual may be admitted with a two-year I-94 even though the visa may be valid for a lesser time. For example, a person with one week left on his E visa may still obtain a two-year I-94 upon entry to the U.S. I have seen this but personally would not feel comfortable with an expired visa. I feel this is just a grey area and an area the NCIS will soon cover.

•   For Canadians, it is especially important to keep in mind that since they are NOT EXEMPT from applying for an E-1 visa, if they change status internally and depart, they will not be readmitted at the POE without first applying for the E-1 visa at a U.S. Consulate. This could be a costly inconvenience because it may delay their reentry by a month or longer.

•   Just because you have your Visa, You can still be turned down at the port of entry if the customs officer suspects something, it is very rare, but keep it in mind, be nice to the immigration officer.

Features of the E-1 Visa

•   The Immigration and Nationality Act (INA) and immigration regulations define an E-1 Visa visitor as someone:

•   Entitled to enter the United States under the provisions of a treaty between the United States and the foreign state of which he or she is a national;

•   Coming to the U.S. solely to carry on trade of a substantial nature, including trade in services or trade in technology;

•   Working either individually or as an employee of a foreign person or organization;

•   Engaged in trade that is international in scope and principally between the United States and the foreign state of which he or she is a national; and

•   The individual intends to depart the United States upon the expiration or termination of E-1 Visa treaty trader status.

Requirements for the E-1 Visa

•   To qualify for E-1 Visa status, the treaty trader must engage in trade between the U.S. and an Authorized E-1 Visa Treaty Country.

•   The trade must be based on an existing relationship involving the international exchange of items. For example, the parties have already entered into successfully negotiated contracts prior to the time of the E-1 Visa application.

• The E-Visa treaty trader's business must conduct over 50% of its international trade with the U.S. A common example of this scenario is where goods are manufactured in Canada and shipped to the U.S. facility for marketing and selling them in the U.S.

• The remainder of the trade (which must constitute less than 50%) may be conducted as domestic or international trade with other countries. As long as more than 50% is conducted between the foreign country and the United States, the remainder is of no consequence with respect to E-1 Visa eligibility.

The definition of "trade" for E-1 Visa requirements is expansive.

• Exchange - There must be an actual exchange of goods or services between the foreign country and the United States. The exchange must be documented and identifiable.

• International - The trade must be international in scope and occur between the foreign country and the United States. The purpose of trade agreements is to encourage trade between the two countries. Therefore, simply doing business in the U.S. without any activity or trade with the foreign country will not suffice for an E-1 visa.

• Qualifying Activities - Trade involves the commercial exchange of goods or services between the foreign country and the United States. Examples of trade of services for E-1 visa purposes includes international banking, insurance, transportation, tourism, communications, newsgathering, consulting, advertising and accounting design and engineering.

In order to qualify for an E-1 Visa, the treaty trader must engage in substantial trade.

- A continuous flow of international trade between the United States and the treaty country.
- Numerous transactions over time. Please note single transactions will not qualify.
- If involved in a small business, the income from international transactions must be sufficient enough to support the treaty trader and his or her family.
- Sources of proof include bills of lading, customer receipts, letters of credit, insurance papers documenting commodities imported, purchase orders, trade brochures, and sales contracts.

Application for an E-1 Visa.

As stated before, you need to contact an immigration attorney. Without one your chances are greatly reduced in being successful. Don't try and do it on a budget, moving to the United States is a big move. You may be planning to take your family, a new home, school, career is hard enough to adapt too. When you add the stress of living in a new country the last thing you want is to have your application turned down in the last minute due to a technicality.

First Step: Application

- Basic application package for a nonimmigrant visa:
  o Form DS-156, Nonimmigrant Visa Application;

o   Form DS-158, Contact Information and Work History for Nonimmigrant Visa Applicant;

o   A valid, unexpired passport;

o   Passport-type photograph; and

o   Application fee, if any.

o   Note that males between the age of 16 and 45 must also use Form DS-157.

Second Step: Inspection at U.S. Port of Entry.

(Note Miami is traditionally very slow at the process; I always try to avoid this port of entry)

- Admission of E-1 Visa: Treaty Trader.

  o   If the E-1 Visa is granted, the E-1 Visa Visitor may then be admitted to the United States by an immigration officer at a U.S. port of entry.

- Duration of E-1 Visa Status.

  o   An E-1 Visa treaty trader may be admitted for an initial period of not more than 2 years.

  o   An E-1 Visa treaty trader generally may not be admitted for a period of time extending more than 6 months beyond the expiration date of his or her passport.

Extension of E-1 Visa

- Extensions of E-1 Visa status may be granted in increments of two years, and may be obtained through a CIS Service Center by filing Form I-129 and the E Supplement.

- There is no limitation on the number of extensions of stay that may be granted.

- To qualify for an extension of stay, the E-1 Visa treaty trader must prove that he or she:

  o Has at all times maintained the terms and conditions of his or her E-Visa nonimmigrant classification;

  o Was physically present in the United States at the time of filing the application for extension of stay; and

  o Has not abandoned his or her extension request.

- Time limit for Certain Employees with Special Qualifications:

  o Employees of business enterprises with special qualifications who are responsible for start-up operations should be able to complete their objectives within 2 years.

  o Absent special circumstances, such employees will not be eligible to obtain an extension of stay.

QUESTIONS & ANSWERS for the E-1 Visa

Q. Does the trading company have to pre-exist.

Answer: Trade must already be established at the time of visa application. Investments, however, may be prospective, provided that the funds are irrevocably committed to the investment, contingent only upon the issuance of the visa. Investment funds may come from any country, including the United States, as long as they are controlled by the investor applicant.

Q. What is substantial trade?

Answer: Substantial trade contemplates a continuous flow of trade items between the US and the treaty country. This means numerous transactions rather than a single transaction regardless of monetary value.

Q. What is a substantial amount of capital?

Answer: There is no fixed amount which is considered "substantial." A substantial amount of capital constitutes that amount which is ample to ensure the investor's financial commitment to the successful operation of the enterprise as measured by the proportionality test. The proportionality test compares the total amount invested in the enterprise with the cost of establishing a viable enterprise of the nature contemplated or the amount of capital needed to purchase an existing enterprise.

Such comparison constitutes the percentage of the treaty applicant's investment in the enterprise. That percentage must compare favorably in the fashion of an inverted sliding scale starting with a high percentage of investment for a lower cost enterprise. The percentage of investment decreases at a gradual rate as the cost of the business increases. An amount of capital invested in an enterprise is merely presumed to be substantial when it meets or exceeds the percentage figures given in the following examples (amounts shown are in US dollars):

75% investment in an enterprise costing but no more than $500,000 (if the cost of the enterprise is substantially lower than $500,000, 85-90%, or even 100% investment may be required).

Plus more than enough income to provide a living for the investor, family and other alien employees.

Q. Are there any travel restrictions on E-1 visa?

Answer: No, there are no travel restrictions on E-1 visa. You may travel as many number of times as required before the expiry of your E-1 status. The USCIS does not impose any time limit on your stay abroad.

Q. What are the limitations of E-1 visa?

Answer: You are restricted to working only for the specific employer or self-owned business that acted as your E-1 visa sponsor. Visas are available only to foreign nationals of countries having trade treaties with the U.S. Visas are approved for two years at a time which makes the application or extension process cumbersome

50% investment in an enterprise costing more than $500,000 but no more than $3,000,000.

30% investment in any enterprise costing more than $3,000,000.

A multi-million dollar investment by a large foreign corporation is normally considered substantial, regardless of the examples given above.

The investment must do more than merely yield a return capable of supporting the investor and family. A marginal enterprise is an enterprise which does not have the capacity to generate significantly more

Q. How long can I stay in the U.S. on E-1 visa?

Answer: You may stay in the U.S. on a prolonged basis with unlimited five year visa extensions or two year status extensions as long as you maintain E-1 qualifications. You may apply for unlimited extensions as long as you are qualified for an E-1 visa.

Q. Can I revalidate my E-1 visa?

Answer: No, you may not apply for visa revalidation of your E-1 visa by mail without leaving the U.S.

Q. Can I bring my dependents on E-1 visa?

Answer: Yes, you may bring your spouse and unmarried children under the age of 21 years to stay along with you. They may stay in the U.S. as long as you maintain your E-1 status. You may bring a domestic or personal servant on nonimmigrant status, provided you can show that. He or she is not abandoning his or her residence abroad and he or she has served you for at least one year, or has had an ongoing employment relationship with you and has at least one year of experience as a servant.

Q. Can my dependents work on E-1 visa?

Answer: Yes, your spouse may seek employment by applying for Employment Authorization using Form I-765, Application for Employment Authorization.

Q. Must the trading company exist and or the investments applied before the visa is issued?

Answer: Trade must already be established at the time the E1 visa application is filed. Investments, however, may be prospective, provided that the funds are irrevocably committed to the investment, contingent only upon the issuance of the visa. Investment funds may come from any country, including the U.S., as long as they are controlled by the investor applicant.

Q. Are joint ventures permitted?

Answer: Yes, provided that the business or individual investor applying for the visa is in a position to "develop and direct" the enterprise. The applicant is in such a position by controlling the enterprise through ownership of at least 50% of the business, possessing operational control through a marginal position or other corporate device, or by other means showing the applicant controls the enterprise.

Section 15) E-2 Visa's (Treaty Visas).

The E-2 Visa is the most common visa applied for those without special skills and degrees. You do have to make a substantial investment, as a rule of thumb, the amount you invest should be Approx $150,000. However it's a grey area and some have been accepted for as little as $50,000 investment.

What sort of Investment / Business?

The investor has to buy a business or invest in a business that gives at least 50% ownership. Investment activities include purchase of a new business.

"The investment must be significantly proportional to the total investment, that is, usually more than half the total value of the enterprise or, if a new business, an amount normally considered necessary to establish the business".

Throughout the United States many small businesses are owned by E-2 Visa holders. Typically an investor would by an established business, say a Maid Service, Gas Station/Garage, Lawn Service Company or Hair Salon. These businesses will typically sell for $75,000-$500,000 US. They come with staff (A requirement) and customers. It is possible to start a brand new business and buy a franchise for example, but considering 40% of all new businesses go under in the first 2 years, a problem that's confounded as you are new to the country, it's safer to buy an established business with a proven track record and Tax returns. Some businesses are 'absentee owner' so you do not have to be running the business on a day to day basis if you have a good manager and staff. Although this type of business will be more expensive.

The business should have, or will have, according to the visa regulations, the capacity to generate more than enough income to support the investor and family. The potential of the business and the credentials of the investor, however, may have a significant bearing on the outcome of a visa application. Net owner income from the business (including net profit, owner's salary) might be as high as $70,000 per annum, but some businesses with owner income as low as $28,000 may also qualify depending on the circumstances, e.g. if there are many employees, or if the investment is particularly large. Various American Embassies throughout the world also vary quite significantly in the standards they apply and so this needs to be discussed with your immigration attorney handling the application. There should be at least two current full time employees or equivalent part time employees (or if it can be shown that the investment in some way has a significant impact on the local economy, then this could also be enough to satisfy). If there are no current employees but the business profits can clearly support employees (and a good case can be made that the seller WILL employ new workers), this can also qualify, but again talk to your immigration attorney who will guide you through the process. If possible the business should have two years' business tax returns which will demonstrate how the business is generating sufficient net income to qualify the buyer for an E-2 Visa and employ U.S workers. A relatively new business for which two years' returns may not be available can still qualify, if anticipated profits and employment can be shown with accountant's projections. The business should have premises from which to operate. Normally this will involve landlord's confirmation that an existing lease can be assigned to the new owner. Although some businesses are run from home, as long as you can show this and your plans, this may be accepted.

There is not really any 'type of business" that has an advantage over another. There are no rules, as to what type of business is can be used. You have to find a business that you feel comfortable with, that you can afford to buy and that's in the area where you want to move too. Once you have done this the fun starts.

First you have to make an offer: In the United States you should never pay the ticket price, ALWAYS put in an offer for a home or business and go at least 10-15% lower, You can always go higher. Never, Ever worry about offending anyone, *it's just business*. Your offer will also have to include that you will buy the business once your Visa application is accepted. Once you and the seller have agreed a price your money must be placed 'at risk' this means in an escrow account. (Normally with the business broker or an attorney) Once you have done this, there is no pulling out. Once your visa application has been accepted, you will have to close on the business, normally within 30 days, or whatever you have in your contract. Once you land in the United States you will then be issued with your 1-94 Card by customs immigration officer.

Its normal practice to ask the existing business owner to stay on for a month and break you in gently, this way you can get to know the day to day routine and suppliers etc.

QUESTIONS & ANSWERS for the E-2 Visa

Q. What is an E-2 Visa?

Answer: The E-2 is a visa for foreign investors (and certain employees of the investor) who are nationals of qualifying countries and who are making a qualifying investment in the United States. The investor may either be an individual or an entity.

Q. How do I qualify for E-2 visa?

Answer: Applicants for E-2 visas must prove three essential elements in order to qualify for an E-2 visa: The investor must have treaty status. The investment must be "substantial" and must result in an active and operating enterprise, plus employee applicants for the E-2 visa must be of the same nationality as the principal investor and either perform duties at the director/manager level or have special qualifications that make his or her skills essential to the operation of the enterprise. Your nationals own at least 50 per cent of the stock of your company i.e. the firm has the nationality of the treaty country. You are investing or your company has invested substantial amount that is at risk, meaning subject to potential loss if the business does not succeed, in a bona fide enterprise in the U.S.

Q. How do you determine whether an applicant has the Correct Treaty Status?

Answer: If the applicant is an individual, then that individual must be a national of a country that has a "treaty of commerce and navigation" or a "bilateral investment treaty" in place with the United States. *See list on previous pages.* If the "Applicant" is a foreign company, then that company must be at least 50% owned by nationals of the same treaty company. Companies that are publicly traded generally are considered to have the nationality of the country where its stock was initially listed on a public stock exchange.

Q. What is a 'substantial investment'?

Answer: An investment of at least $150,000 is considered substantial. However, it is not fixed and there are a few consulates which accept as low as $50,000. Ideally $150,000 would be the most appropriate figure. *These figures are not the regulations of the USCIS, but they reflect my experience in these cases over the years.* If you wish to invest $500,000 or greater then you may wish to petition for permanent immigration, *see the following pages for details.* Theoretically an investment of $1 million or even $100 million will not guarantee one will qualify for the E-2, though it should improve your chances quite significantly.

Q. What are the limitations of E-2 visa?

Answer: E-2 visas are available only to nationals of countries having trade treaties with the United States. E-2 visas are approved for Five to two years at a time which makes the application/extension process cumbersome and expensive. You are restricted to work only for the specific employer or self-owned business that acted as your E-2 visa sponsor.

Q. What privileges do I enjoy on E-2 visa and how long can I stay?

Answer: You are travel freely in and out of the U.S. Work legally in the company that is the investment vehicle in the United States. You can also bring your dependents or accompanying relatives and your spouse may also work while in the United States. Stay on a prolonged basis with unlimited two year extensions as long as you maintain E-2 qualifications and don't incur a criminal record. There is no limit on the number of extensions you can take.

Q. How do I apply for extension of stay on E-2 visa?

Answer: For an E-2 extension you must submit Form I-129, Petition for Nonimmigrant Worker, along with E

Supplement and submit Form I-539, Application to Extend or Change Nonimmigrant Status, for accompanying relatives. Plus you must include Copy of your personal and U.S. business income tax returns for the past two years, including payroll tax returns, a copy of your complete passport including the original E-2 visa or Copy of original Form I-797, Copy of your Form I-94 Card and if applicable a Copy of your Form I-94 Arrival-Departure document.

Also if you file for extension before the expiry of your I-94 Card you may continue working and running the business for 240 days while waiting for the decision. If you file after the expiry of the visa you may stay up to 40 days awaiting the decision. If there is no decision within the 40 days you must leave terminating your work in the United States.

Q. Are there any travel restrictions on E-2 investor visas?

Answer: The USCIS does not impose any travel restrictions and does not have a time limit on the amount of time you spend abroad. (Unlike the Green Card) You are free to come as go as you please.

Q. Can I change my status while on an E-2 visa?

Answer: Yes, you may apply for change of status while on E-2 visa. You must submit Form I-129, Petition for Nonimmigrant Worker, indicating your change of status with appropriate supporting documents. You can also apply for other visa's and even a Green Card. You can NOT apply for United States Citizenship; to apply you must be a permanent resident. As an E-2 Visa Holder you will be classed as a Non-Resident Temporary Alien. (Temporary Resident). Thus unable to apply for citizenship. A green card holder can apply after 5 years. As a green card holder is classed as a permanent resident, although a green card has to be renewed every 10 years. Please be aware the E-2 status is NOT transferable to a green card, this must be applied for as a different entity. *Please see green cards.*

Q. How about my family?

Answer: The spouse and unmarried children under 21 are entitled to the same E-2 classification as the principal alien. The nationality of the spouse/children is not material to their classification as long as the principal alien is a treaty national. Your spouse may seek employment by applying for Employment Authorization using Form I-765, Application for Employment Authorization. Effective January 16, 20002, dependent spouses of E visa holders are eligible to apply for work authorization from USCIS. Children of E visa holders are not permitted to work in the United States unless they independently qualify for employment authorization, such as an E, H, or L visa

Q. Do I actually need an E visa to reside in the United States if I own a US business?

Answer: Unless you are a U.S. Citizen or a U.S. Green Card holder, you must be in possession of a valid have a visa in order to enter the United States in Treaty Trader or Treaty Investor status. Further, all successful E visa applicants and their dependents are expected to present valid passports in order to be issued the visa, regardless of nationality.

Q. I received a change of status in the United States from U.S. Citizenship and Immigration Services (USCIS). Is that all that I need to present in order to be issued an E visa at the U.S. Embassy or U.S. Consulate?

Answer: Sorry but no. The change of status simply allows you to remain in the United States until the expiration of the status granted. If you have been granted a change of status by USCIS and leave the U.S., you must have an E visa in your passport in order to return to the U.S. in that status. To obtain a visa you must lodge a complete application with the appropriate U.S. Embassy or U.S. Consulate. Adjudication of your case can vary from two weeks to six months, depending on which U.S. Embassy or U.S. Consulate is deciding your case.

Q. Do I need an immigration attorney?

Answer: There is no legal requirement that you hire an attorney to lodge your E visa application. While many E Visa applicants choose to retain the services of an attorney to aid in the preparation of their case, others do not. It is to your advantage, however, to engage the services of a competent immigration attorney or law firm that is fully familiar with the specific procedures observed by the U.S. Embassy or U.S. Consulate in your home country. Failure to observe these procedures will certainly result in significant time delays, may seriously prejudice the outcome of your case, and may result in irreversible financial consequences.

Q. Can I study on E-2 visa?

Answer? Yes, you may study on E-2 Visa; however, you may not join a full length program like an F-1. You may take up a few credits at a university when they do not harm the primary interest of the visa. Plus your dependents may join U.S. schools, colleges and universities, and do not have to apply for separate student visa such as an F-1 visa.

Q. Can my fiancé (e), common law or same-sex partner accompany me with the E-2 Visa?

Answer: Under U.S. immigration law, a legal marriage must exist before one is considered to be a spouse. Therefore, fiancé (e) s, common law or same-sex partners do not qualify for derivative E visa status. Other avenues may be available to assist those applicants in such a situation. Please contact our firm for more details.

Q. Will I have to appear before the U.S. Embassy or U.S. Consulate in person?

Answer: For all categories of visas, including Treaty Visas, each applicant age 14 or older must appear for a personal interview before a Consular Officer. In all cases, each applicant (including those under 14 years of age), must be physically present in the country of application at the time of issuance. Those applicants who are found to be ineligible for a U.S. visa for criminal convictions, immigration violations, drug charges, or other similar reasons may have to appear to determine grounds of ineligibility and applicability of a waiver for any such ineligibility. In such cases the applicant must be prepared for a wait of up to 180 days while eligibility is confirmed and/or a waiver requested.

Q. How do I apply for E2 visa?

Answer: Completed and signed Form DS-156, Nonimmigrant Visa Application, Completed and signed Form DS-156E,

Treaty or Trader Investor Application, A letter from your employer detailing your position and stating that you possess highly specialized skills essential for the efficient operation of the firm, Documents that establishing the nationality of your company, Evidence of investment in the United States, Any other documents relevant to the case such as marriage and birth certificates of you and your family members, Two photographs (37 x 37mm) for each member listed in the visa application. The picture should be taken before a light background and without head covering and of course a passport valid for travel to the U.S and with validity dates at least six months beyond your intended period of stay.

Q. My spouse and/or children are citizens of a country other than my own. Can they still accompany me?

Answer: The spouse and children (defined as unmarried and less than 21 years of age) do not need to have the same citizenship as the principal applicant. However, dependents of E visa holders are required to have visas in order to accompany the principal applicant to the U.S.

Q. Where do I file my E-2 visa application?

Answer: If you are in a lawful status in the U.S., submit the visa application to a USCIS field office in the United States. But if you are outside the United States, submit the visa application to the U.S. consular office in your home country.

Q. What is the processing time for E2 visas?

Answer: The processing time for E2 visas is generally between two weeks to 6 months from the filing of the application, however, it may take longer in some Consular posts. This may vary depending upon the work load in the U.S. Consulate you choose to apply. In Mexico it can go through in 1 week, The UK it will take up to six months.

Q. I am a citizen of Australia presently residing in the United Kingdom. Must I lodge my E-2 visa application in the United Kingdom or in Australia?

Answer: A citizen of one of the other qualifying treaty countries who is resident in the United Kingdom may lodge an E visa application at the U.S. Embassy in London. In the case of a citizen of Australia, filing in Australia is permitted and may save significant processing time. But however in contrast, a citizen of Spain living in the United Kingdom is not presently allowed to file an E-2 visa application in his homeland Spain.

Q. What is the history behind the E-2 visa?

Answer: The United States Congress created a provision in the Immigration and Nationality Act of 1952 permitting certain foreign nationals who invested in the United States to obtain a temporary work visa, now known as the E-2 visa, "to develop and direct the...enterprise which he or she has invested." The United States had to have a treaty with the country the foreign national was from, now most commonly called a bilateral investment treaty. Today, there are over 50 foreign countries that have signed treaties with the United States. Not only do individual investors qualify for the visa, but also certain employees of businesses who are investing in the United States may also qualify

Q .My wife and I are both holding E-2 visas in the United States. Our son was born in the US in 2005 and thus is an

American citizen. Are we qualified for green card because of him? Could we apply before he is 18?

Answer: Your child cannot petition for you to get a green card by virtue of his being a US citizen until he is 21 years old. Once he is 21, he / she can apply on your behalf and close relative.

Q. What happens if I later sell my business?

Answer: If you sell the business without previously buying another qualifying business, you are no longer eligible to remain in E-2 status. You must either leave the States, or apply to change to a different status, for which you do qualify.

Q. What happens if I have a criminal conviction?

Answer: Don't, but If you have a conviction, or have been arrested, this has to be stated in the visa application and a Memorandum of Conviction obtained from the Court in question. Eligibility will depend on the nature of the conviction. Minor offences such as traffic violations may not cause a problem.

Q. Are joint ventures permitted?

Answer: Yes, provided that the business or individual investor applying for the visa is in a position to "develop and direct" the enterprise. The applicant is in such a position by controlling the enterprise through ownership of at least 50% of the business, possessing operational control through a marginal position or other corporate device, or by other means showing the applicant controls the enterprise.

E-2 Visa Benefits

You can travel freely in and out of the U.S. while on a valid E2 visa

You can live and work legally in the U.S. for a U.S. company that is the subject of the investment

Your spouse may seek employment by applying for an employment authorization document

You may bring your dependents (spouse and unmarried children under the age of 21) to live with you in the U.S.

You can stay on a prolonged basis with unlimited two year extensions as long as you maintain valid E2 Visa status.

Your children can attend school for no cost. (Unless you send them to a private school, see Education)

Section 16) E-3 Visa's.

E-3 Visa

The E-3 Visa is a new visa category only for Australians going to the U.S. to work temporarily in a specialty occupation. It is ONLY for citizens of Australia, who have a legitimate offer of employment in the U.S. Plus the position you are coming to fill qualifies as specialty occupation employment. You have the necessary academic or other qualifying credentials. An approved Labor Condition Application is required and no more than 10,500 E-3 visas can be issued per year.

How to apply

Submit a job offer letter from the prospective United States-based employer. A treaty alien in a specialty occupation must meet the general academic and occupational requirements for the position pursuant to INA 214(i)(1). In addition to the nonimmigrant visa application, the following documentary evidence must be submitted in connection with an application for an E-3 visa: A certified Form ETA 9035 clearly annotated as 'E-3 - Australia - to be processed.

Evidence of academic or other qualifying credentials are required under INA 214(i)(1), and a job offer letter or other documentation from the employer establishing that upon entry into the U.S. you will be engaged in qualifying work in a specialty occupation and that you will be paid the actual or prevailing wage referred to in INA 212(t)(1). A certified copy of the foreign degree and evidence that it is equivalent to the required U.S. degree could be used to satisfy the 'qualifying credentials' requirement. Likewise, a certified copy of a U.S. baccalaureate or higher degree, as required by the specialty occupation, would meet the minimum evidentiary standard. If you don't have an academic or other qualifying credential. Then you will need evidence of education and experience that is equivalent to the required U.S. degree, Plus evidence that your stay will ONLY be temporary. A certified copy of any required license or other official permission to practice the occupation in the state of intended employment if so required or, where licensure is not necessary to commence immediately the intended specialty occupation employment upon admission, evidence that the alien will be obtaining the required license within a reasonable time after admission. If required before you may commence employment in the specialty occupation. Plus that you have the necessary license or other official permission to practice in the specialty occupation.

A specialty occupation is one that requires the attainment of a bachelor's or higher degree in the specific specialty (or its equivalent) as a minimum for entry into the occupation in the U.S. In determining whether an occupation qualifies as a 'specialty occupation', follow the definition contained at INA 214 for H-1B non-immigrants and applicable standards and criteria determined by the Department of Homeland Security (DHS) and USCIS.

Remember that An E-3 alien must meet academic and occupational requirements, including licensure where appropriate, for admission into the U.S. in a specialty occupation. If the job requires licensure or other official permission to perform the specialty occupation, the applicant must submit proof of the requisite license or permission before the E-3 visa may be granted. In certain cases, where such a license or other official permission is not immediately required to perform the duties described in the visa application, you must show that you will obtain such licensure within a reasonable period of time following admission to the U.S.

Unlike other petitions, you employer is not required to submit a petition to the Department of Homeland Security as a prerequisite for visa issuance. But the Visa can be Labor Condition Application ETA Form 9035, from the Department of Labor. The E-3 Visa is valid renewed. If you are on an E-3 Visa, your spouse is permitted to work in the United States, but first they must apply with the Department of Homeland Security and apply using Form I-765.

E-3 Visa Facts.

No upper age limit. . You need to have a job offer from the U.S. before you can apply for the E-3 visa. You cannot apply for an E-3 visa from within the U.S. However you can travel on the Visa Waiver Program (VWP) if you meet the requirements (please see our page on the Visa Waiver Program). If you do not meet the VWP requirements, you may be eligible to travel on the B-1/B-2 Combined Visa for Business or Pleasure. You can apply at any U.S. Embassy or Consulate which processes nonimmigrant petition-based visas, but you cannot apply from within the U.S. Other than the normal non-refundable worldwide visa application fee of US$100, there is no special fee for an E-3 visa. E-3 spouses are entitled to work in the United States and may apply for an Employment Authorization Document (Form I-765) through U.S. Citizenship and Immigration Service (USCIS). The spouse of a qualified E nonimmigrant may, upon admission to the United States, apply with the Department of Homeland Security for an employment authorization document, which an employer could use to verify the spouse's employment eligibility. Such spousal employment may be in a position other than a specialty occupation. Please note however that the U.S. does not recognize De Facto relationships or same-sex Civil Partnerships for the purposes of immigration, and to qualify as a spouse you will need a marriage certificate from the Department of Births, Deaths and Marriages.

You can enter the U.S. 10 days before you start your job. And you can stay 10 days after you finish your job. An E-3 visa is a multiple-entry visa, so provided you have not changed employers or made any other changes to your immigration status, you may travel outside the U.S. and reenter on a valid, unexpired E-3 visa, Plus there is no limit to how long you can stay outside the U.S. or how many times you can travel outside the U.S. during the validity of your E-3 visa. In Australia, if an E-3 visa is approved at interview, it is normally issued within 2-3 business days. Visas and passports are returned by mail, so please also allow time for this. Applicants should bring a self-addressed registered or express post envelope to the interview.

Section 17) E-5 Visa's.

The EB-5 Visa offers a great opportunity for people who wish to move to the United States and become permanent residents. A person investing $500,000 in certain circumstances or $1 million in a business that creates 10 jobs may be granted EB-5 permanent resident status. The government criteria for this excellent status are that the investment must be in a business and not just an investment in the stock market. The invested funds must be the individual's, but may be a gift from a parent or other person, provided the appropriate gift taxes are paid, if required; Lawfully gained.

Also the business must have been created after November 29, 1990 or the investment must substantially change an older business.

Commercial Enterprise: Any for profit business can qualify, including sole proprietorships, limited or general partnerships, corporations, business trusts, joint ventures, holding companies and wholly owned for-profit commercial subsidiaries, mutual investment funds, etc. An existing commercial enterprise purchased by you can also qualify without necessity for reorganization or reincorporating, if your infusion of capital increases the business' net worth or the number of qualifying U.S. workers employed by 40%. Pre-existing commercial enterprises also qualify if you save ten U.S. jobs by taking over a troubled business that has operated for-at-least two years and has incurred a net loss of at least 20% of net worth during one of the two years preceding your investment.

The amount of investment may be $500,000 in a rural or high unemployment area; and Create 10 jobs – no direct job creation is required if the investment is in a Regional Center.

To encourage immigration through the EB5 Investor Green Card category, Congress created a Regional Center program in 1993. 3,000 visas have been set aside each year for people who invest at least $500,000 in designated Regional Centers. This particular program does not require the immigrant investor enterprise itself to employ 10 U.S. workers. Instead, it is sufficient if 10 or more jobs are created indirectly as a result of the investment.

The Regional Centers program does not require the immigrant investor enterprise itself to employ 10 U.S. workers. Instead, it is sufficient if 10 or more jobs are created indirectly as a result of the investment. Regional Centers are designated as "any economic unit, public or private, which is involved with the promotion of economic growth, including increased export sales, improved regional productively, job creation, or increased domestic capital investment." The investment requirement is only $500,000 if a Regional Center is in a targeted employment area, which is either in a rural or high unemployment area, as defined hereinafter in the section on EB-5 Regulations. In 2003, Congress gave CIS (formerly INS) discretion to "give priority" to EB-5 petitions filed through a Regional Center. Once Permanent Resident status is granted, minimal involvement with the investment is permitted, allowing the applicant to work in any business, go to school, or enjoy retirement.

Location: After Hurricane Katrina hit the area of New Orleans, LA became such an area. The only location criteria apply to $500,000 investments in targeted employment areas, which include rural areas identified by the U.S. census or the Office of Management and Budget and areas certified by a State government to be experiencing average unemployment of at least 150% of the national average. These rural areas, defined as any area other than one within a metropolitan statistical area or within the boundary of a city or town with a population of 20,000 or more;

EB-5 Permanent Resident status involves making the investment, filing the appropriate petition at a CIS Service Center, and applying for an Immigrant Visa at a United States consulate or applying for Adjustment of Status in the U.S. After "Conditional" Resident Status (Green Card) is granted, the individual must wait one year and nine months to file an application to remove the "conditional" status. With this application, evidence of the creation of the 10 jobs, if necessary, is required as well as proof the entire investment has been made. Upon approval of the application by CIS, the applicant is granted Permanent Resident status. You must be engaged in management of the enterprise, either through daily managerial control or through policy formulation as a corporate officer, director, or partner.

Multiple Investors: Each multiple investor in the same enterprise will qualify if he or she meets the minimal capital and job creation requirements. In cases where not all multiple investors seek to immigrate to the United States based on the investment, the job creation requirement can be met by those investors who seek to immigrate (based on the joint investment) by apportioning the total number of jobs created among the immigrating investors rather than among all investors. (Note: This apportionment among joint investors does not apply to the capital requirement.) However each investor must create at least 10 jobs for US workers.

To apply you may petition for yourself, by filing USCIS Form I-526 at the USCIS service area that has with jurisdiction over the location of the business. Although this is currently in Texas and California. Once your petition is approved, you will receive conditional immigrant status. You must apply to remove conditional status during the 90 days <u>before </u>the second anniversary of the date you received this status, if not you will automatically lose your permanent resident status. You need to file Form I-829 to have the conditions removed. Your business and investment will be re-examined to determine compliance with regulatory requirements, including capital committed and employment created

There are 10,000 EB-5 Visa's issued each year. Some are denied for document errors. I would suggest you seek an attorney who specializes in EB-5 Visa's. Why take the chance?

Questions for EB-5 Visa

Do I have to have previous business experience?

Answer: No

Do I have to be able to speak English?

Answer: No

What is meant by the investment being lawfully gained?

Answer: You have to prove that the investment is from a lawful business, investments, salary, bonus, sale of a home, gift or inheritance.

Who receives the Green card?

Answer: Applicant, spouse and unmarried children under 21.

Is the EB-5 Visa a truly passive investment?

Answer: *That's a good question*: The EB-5 Visa regulations require involvement in management or policy making. The regulations deem a limited partner in a limited partnership that conforms to the Uniform Limited Partnership Act as sufficiently engaged in the EB-5 enterprise. However, the Uniform Limited Partnership, adopted by most states of the United States, prohibits the limited partner from actively participating in management!

Is my investment safe and risk free?

Answer: No. The law requires an "at risk" investment without guarantees.

How long does INS take to process my visa petition?

Answer: From 7 -15 months. On average 10 months.

Can money gifted by a parent or other relative be used for an EB-5 investment?

Answer: Yes, provided that any applicable gift taxes are paid. However it must be demonstrated that the gift is an actual arms length transaction and is a not a mere ruse or that the gifted funds will be given back after permanent resident status is granted.

Are EB-5 visas available to people from any country in the world?

Answer: Yes.

Section 18) L- Visa's.

The United States L1 visa is a non-immigrant visa which allows companies operating both in the US and abroad to transfer certain classes of employee from its foreign operations to the USA operations for up to seven years. The employee must have worked for a subsidiary, parent, affiliate or branch office of your US Company outside of the US for at least one year out of the last three years.

Companies operating in the US can apply to the relevant BCIS service center for an L1 visa to transfer someone to the US from their overseas operations. Employees in this category will, initially, be granted an L-1 visa for up to three years. If you have a company example Real Estate/ Estate Agent in your home country, you can apply to run a subsidiary in the United States, You will have course have to apply and pass local real estate license and comply with local and state laws and certification.

There are two types of employees who may be sponsored for USA L1 visas:

• Managers/Executives

The legal definition of management and executive roles for these purposes is quite strict, and a detailed description of the duties attached to the position will be required. In particular, the executive or manager should have supervisory responsibility for professional staff and/or for a key function, department or subdivision of the employer. Such personnel are issued an L1A visa, initially for a three year period extendible in two year increments to a maximum of seven years.

- **Specialized Knowledge Staff**

This category covers those with knowledge of the company's products/services, research, systems, proprietary techniques, management, or procedures. Staff in this category are issued an L1B visa, initially for three years extendible to a maximum of five years.

On completing the maximum allowable period in L-1 status, the employee must be employed outside the United States for a minimum of one year before a new application is made for L or H status.

L-1 Advantages

The major advantage to the L-1 visa is that certain applicants qualifying for this visa may also qualify for faster Green Card processing. L-1 foreign nationals who are managers and executives are eligible for the "priority workers" category. Foreign nationals falling into this category may apply for permanent residency without having to undergo the time consuming labor certification process.

L-1 Visa Questions and Answers

Q. What is L-1 visa?

Answer: The L-1 visa category was established to facilitate the transfer or rotation of foreign personnel of an international company into the United States. Although originally targeted toward large U.S. multinational corporations, this is an appropriate method for companies of all sizes to seek immediate immigration benefits for their qualifying employees. Further, the L-1 visa may provide quick access to lawful permanent resident (immigrant) status in the United States. In layman terms, if you or your family-run a business in your home country, you can apply to open a similar business in the United States as a subsidiary.

Q. How do I qualify for L-1 Visa?

Answer: The U.S. Company to which you are being transferred must be a branch, subsidiary, affiliate or joint venture partner of your non-U.S. employer and Employment in the U.S. Company must be as a manager, executive or person with specialized knowledge and skills. Although originally targeted toward large U.S. multinational corporations, this is an appropriate method for companies of all sizes to seek immediate immigration benefits for their qualifying employees.

Q. What are the limitations of L-1 visa?

Answer: An L-1 petition may be approved initially for up to three years, with the possibility of extension for up to four more years. In the case of a "new office" in the U.S., the L-1 will be limited to one year initially with extensions provided thereafter if the new office flourishes. You can get visa approval for up to three years. Extensions of two years at a time may be allowed until you have been in the U.S. for a total of seven years if you are a manager or executive, five years if you come as a specialized knowledge employee.

Q. What is the difference between L-1A visa and L-1B visa?

Answer: The L-1A visa is for managers and executives. On L-1A visa you may apply for a Green Card without going through the process of Labor Certification. If you were a manager or executive with the overseas branch for one year, you do not have to be in L-1A status for a year unless you are starting a new company in the U.S. after being on L-1 status for only a year.

The L-1B visa is only for key employees. You must have specialized knowledge of the company's products or procedures.

Q. Can I extend my stay on L-1 visa?

Answer: Yes, you may apply for L1 visa extension using Form I-129, and L Supplement. Extensions of two years at a time may be allowed until you have been in the U.S. for a total of seven years if you are a manager or executive.

Q. Do you need a lawyer to get an L-1 visa?

Answer: No, but as already mentioned in this book, it is well worth it.

Q. How long does it take to process an L-1 Visa?

Answer: It can be dealt with in 2 – 4 months to process. But the USCIS has instituted a program called Premium Processing. If the USCIS is paid an extra $1,000 on a separate check, the USCIS guarantees it will adjudicate the petition in 15 days or notify you if more evidence is needed.

Q. What are the minimum educational requirements or business experience for an Executive or Manager to get L-1 visa?

Answer: There is no Minimum Education requirement, but you must have work at the same position

Q. If one is on an L-2 (dependent visa), is it possible to obtain a work permit based on this status?

Answer: Yes because in January of 2002, the law changed allowing L2 dependents to obtain work authorization. An L2 holder may apply for the Employment Authorization Card (EAD) form an INS Service Center.

<u>Section 19)</u> The Green Card Form I-551.

A United States Permanent Resident Card, Known simply as the Green Card is an identification card for lawful permanent resident of the United States.

Green Card also refers to a process of becoming a Lawful Permanent Residence. The Green Card serves as proof that is holder has permission to reside (Under certain conditions) and work in the United States. The holder must maintain resident status by residing in the United States and can be removed. It is called Green card as the predecessor form I-151 that was introduced at the end of World War II was printed on green paper. The new form I-551 was adopted in 1977 and is now printed on paper of various colors.

Green cards were formerly issued by the Immigration and naturalization Service (INS). That agency has been replaced by the Bureau of Citizenship and Immigration Service (BCIS). It is also part of the Department of Homeland Security (DHS). Shortly after re-organization BCIS was renamed to U.S Citizenship and Immigration Services. (USCIS).

The following may obtain a 'Green Card' without 'Labor Certification'

Aliens of Extraordinary Ability in Business, Sciences, Arts, Education, or Athletics

Outstanding Professors/Researchers

International Executives/Managers

Exceptional Ability in the Sciences, Arts, Business with a "National Interest Waiver"

Registered Physical Therapists

Registered Professional Nurses

Aliens of Exceptional Ability in Business, Sciences, Arts, or Education.

Applications for a 'Green Card' for aliens of exceptional ability should be supported by:

Labor certification - unless waived (see above),

AND: at least 3 (and preferably more) of the following:

An official academic record showing that the candidate has a degree, diploma, or certificate,

OR: A Similar award from an institution of learning relating to the area of exceptional ability;

Letter(s) from current or former employers showing that the candidate has at least 10 years of full-time experience in the occupation for which he/she is being sought;

A license to practice the profession or certification for a particular profession or occupation;

Evidence that the alien has commanded a salary, or other remuneration for services, which demonstrates exceptional ability;

Evidence of membership of professional associations;

Evidence of recognition for achievements and significant contributions to the industry of field by peers, Governmental entities, or professional or business organizations.

International Executives and Managers

A multinational corporation with an established US office (i.e. one that has been in existence for at least one year), may obtain a 'Green Card' for international executives who have worked in an executive or managerial capacity for a non-US branch of the corporation for at least one year in the last three.

Applications under this category will generally need to be supported by:

A Letter from the employer confirming employment outside the US, the nature of the previous employment, and the dates of employment.

If relevant, a letter from the US employer confirming the nature of the previous employment, and the dates of employment.

A job description for the prospective employee.

Tax returns showing employment of the candidate by the same employer outside of the U.S. for at least one year in the last three years.

Accounts for the employer in the US.

Professionals with Advanced Degrees

This category is detailed below; it can only be used following 'Labor Certification'

Professionals

This category is detailed below; it can only be used following 'Labor Certification'

Skilled Workers

This category is detailed below; it can only be used following 'Labor Certification'

Other Workers

This category is detailed below; it can only be used following 'Labor Certification'

Labor Certification

Before you may obtain a 'Green Card' for a foreign worker who does not qualify for exemption from 'Labor Certification' (as outlined on the preceding pages), that company must demonstrate to the local office of the US Department of Labor that the job is one for which there are not sufficient United States workers who are willing, qualified, and available at the time of application for a visa.

The employer must also demonstrate that the employment of the foreign worker will not adversely affect the wages and/or working conditions of workers in the United States similarly employed.

Labor Certification is a difficult and time-consuming process, but, in itself, it does not permit an alien to start work in the US. It is simply one of several requirements before for the grant of an immigrant visa.

An application for Labor Certification is made using official form ETA 750; this form comes in two parts.

The Green card is issued for 10 years. A green card holder can re-apply in 10 years. Many people have done this and now are on their fourth application. However as the Green card gives you permanent residence status. After five years you can apply for citizenship. To apply for citizenship it does NOT mean you have to give up your native countries citizenship. You can have dual nationality and carry 2 passports. Carrying two passports is very handy when travelling abroad. It makes passport and border crossing faster.

What if I am on a E-1, E-2 L-1 Visa, can I apply for a green card?

Answer: YES. Here's how.

So you are on an E-2 Visa for example, this is not transferable to a green card. Hundreds of immigration attorneys and so called experts will tell you NO. OK they are partially correct, but let's look at the bigger picture.

If you are here working in the United States running a business, and you have been at it for at least 2 years. What have you got? Experience and you have made some friends and relationships with other businesses similar to yours. It does not matter what sort of business it is, a maid service, a hair salon, a garage, etc.

While the investment that got you your E-2 Visa itself does not help you qualify for a Green Card, being an E-2 Visa holder in no way stops you from getting a Green Card if it can be shown that you qualify under some other category. This is where the third party comes in, your business friends. It is perfectly legal and normal for the employee in question (you) to be legally in the U.S. on a different kind of visa (e.g. E-2 Visa) and have a Labor Certification application pending through an independent third party employer. (Your friend)In this scenario, you would still need to maintain your legal visa status until such time as the Labor Certification process is complete and the final Green Card application has been submitted. In this category, the employer must show that there is a shortage of U.S. employees with the requisite <u>education or experience</u> to fill the position. Therefore for a Green Card through Labor Certification need not necessarily have a Bachelors Degree.

The application is done in 3 phases.

Phase 1 Labor Certification. A 30 day recruitment process must be undertaken by the employer (your friend) to show that your sponsorship is necessary due to the lack of qualified applicants generated by the recruitment campaign. Following the 30 day recruitment campaign the employer has to wait a further 30 days to give people a chance to respond. At the end of the 60 days a 'Labor Certification' application is filed on-line with the Department of State. Approval can normally be obtained within 60 days of filing. The date that the Labor Certification application is filed is known as your "Priority Date".

When the job is advertised it must be done correctly, to show you have tried to attract American employees. You will need to advertise in the largest local Sunday paper, advertise on the company website, a job fair and the notice board at the place of work. All this must be recorded and submitted.

Phase 2 Immigrant Petition. Once the Labor Certification application has been approved, an 'I-140 Immigrant Petition' is filed with USCIS (Immigration). You need to send the approved Labor Certification to USCIS together with a letter from the employer that they still want to hire you plus evidence of their ability to pay the offered wage. The purpose of the Immigrant Petition is to have Immigration 'rubber stamp' that you are indeed eligible for the category that you are applying for. Approval of the Immigrant Petition is usually received in 6-12 months.

Phase 3 Make the application for Green Card. This can be done either at the U.S. Embassy in your home country or in the U.S. provided each family member is in the U.S. on a visa of any kind (e.g. E-2, B-2 or L-1 Visa). Either way processing is likely to be completed and your Green Cards issued in approximately 6 months. However, you can only apply for this third and final stage if there are Green Cards available in the category you are applying for. Immigration only has a limited number of Green Cards available in each category each year and they announced in late 2005 that the category had become massively oversubscribed. When this happens, Immigration announce a 'Priority Date' that they will accept Stage 3 applications for. The application for Green cards must also be made for the spouse and any unmarried children under 21. The path is simple but it has to be a genuine business and you have to prove that you can do the job, however like I said above if you have at least 2 years experience you can do this. Plus when your future employer advertises for the position, it can be worded to fit your Resume / CV. The process is complicated and will cost approx $10,000 if you employ an attorney who can do this. If you try to do this without an immigration attorney with experience in this (and there are not that many) you will most probably fail. In the back of the book, I have listed many websites for such immigration service providers. Please note I am NOT making a recommendation, I receive no funds for listing the contact names, it is just for your reference. Once you have your Green card you are free to work for your friend and if that does not work out, anyone else. Good luck.

<u>Section 20)</u> Citizenship.

All persons born or naturalized in the United States, and subject to the jurisdiction thereof, are citizens of the United States and of the state wherein they reside. No state shall make or enforce any law which shall abridge the privileges or immunities of citizens of the United States; nor shall any state deprive any person of life, liberty, or property, without due process of law; nor deny to any person within its jurisdiction the equal protection of the laws. - XIV Amendment to the U.S. Constitution

Citizenship is one of the most coveted gifts that the United States Government can bestow, and the most important immigration benefit that USCIS can grant.   Most people become U.S. citizens in one of two ways:

• By being born in the United States. (Birth), either within the territory of the United States or to U.S. citizen parents, or by Naturalization.

When a pregnant illegal immigrant, or someone in the United legally (Tourist, visa) when the child is born in the United States, That child is a United States Citizen. The parents can be deported, but the INS has no powers to deport the child. For rules on Citizenship via family member see forward pages on immediate relatives. To apply contact an immigration attorney or follow instructions on the USCIS website. I normally recommend an attorney, however this process is something you might able do yourself. www.uscis.com

• Benefits

• All the rights listed in the Constitution including the right to vote

- Right to have a U.S. passport

- Right to work in the U.S.

How to apply.

Before you apply just check that you meet the following criteria:

You must be 18 or older

You can read, write, and speak Basic English. (Age or disability may allow exemption of this requirement.)

You have been a permanent resident of the U.S., with a Resident Card, for 5 years continuously without leaving for long periods of time.

You must pass a civics exam. See the 100 questions later in the book.

You must be able to swear to be of good moral character.

If male, you must have complied with the Selective Service requirements.

If male, you have never been discharged from armed services for being an alien.

If male, you have never deserted the armed forces.

If male, be willing to serve in the armed forces, if eligible and required.

You must take an oath of allegiance to the U.S.

You must certify that you will uphold the Constitution of the United States.

If married, you have been married to a U.S. citizen for at least 3 years, and the spouse has been a citizen for more than 3 years.

Section 21) 100 Citizen Questions.

When you take your test, you will have 100 questions. Below is a sample of what the questions will be, EACH state will have a slight variation. Applicants for citizenship will have to correctly answer six out of 10 randomly-chosen questions from a new master list of 100.

1. What are the colors of our flag?
   Red, white, and blue

2. How many stars are there in our flag?
   Fifty (50)

3. What color are the stars on our flag?
   White

4. What do the stars on the flag mean?
   One for each state in the union

5. How many stripes are there in the flag?
   Thirteen (13)

6. What color are the stripes?
   Red and white

7. What do the stripes on the flag mean?
   They represent the original 13 states

8. How many states are there in the union?
   Fifty (50)

9. What is the 4th of July?
   Independence Day

10. What is the date of Independence Day?
    July 4th

11. Independence from whom?
    England

12. What country did we fight during the Revolutionary War?
England

13. Who was the first president of the United States?
George Washington

14. Who is the president of the United States today?
George W. Bush

15. Who is the vice president of the United States today?
Dick Cheney

16. Who elects the president of the United States?
The Electoral College

17. Who becomes president of the United States if the president should die?
Vice President

18. For how long do we elect the president?
Four years

19. What is the Constitution?
The supreme law of the land

20. Can the Constitution be changed?
Yes

21. What do we call a change to the Constitution?
Amendments

22. How many changes or amendments are there to the Constitution?
Twenty-seven (27)

23. How many branches are there in our government?
Three (3)

24. What are the three branches of our government?
Legislative, Executive, and Judiciary

25. What is the legislative branch of our government?
Congress

26. Who makes the laws in the United States?
Congress

27. What is Congress?
The Senate and the House of Representatives

28. What are the duties of Congress?
To make laws

29. Who elects Congress?
The people

30. How many senators are there in Congress?
One hundred (100)

31. Can you name the two senators from your state?
Different answers for every state. For California the
answer is Barbara Boxer and Dianne Feinstein

32. For how long do we elect each senator?
6 years

33. How many representatives are there in Congress?
Four hundred thirty-five (435)

34. For how long do we elect the representatives?
2 years

35. What is the executive branch of our government?
The president, Cabinet, and departments under
Cabinet members

36. What is the judiciary branch of our government?
The Supreme Court

37. What are the duties of the Supreme Court?
To interpret laws

38. What is the supreme law of the United States?
The Constitution

39. What is the Bill of Rights?
The first 10 amendments of the Constitution

40. What is the capital of your state?
Different answers for every state. For California the answer is Sacramento

41. Who is the current governor of your state?
Different answers for every state. For California the answer is Arnold Schwarzenegger

42. Who becomes president of the U.S.A. if the president and the vice president should die?
Speaker of the House of Representatives

43. Who is the Chief Justice of the Supreme Court?
John Roberts

44. Can you name the thirteen original states?
Connecticut, New Hampshire, New York, New Jersey, Massachusetts, Pennsylvania, Delaware, Virginia, North Carolina, South Carolina, Georgia, Rhode Island, and Maryland

45. Who said, "Give me liberty or give me death"?
Patrick Henry

46. Which countries were our enemies during World War II?
Germany, Italy, and Japan

47. What are the 49th and 50th states of the union?
Alaska and Hawaii

48. How many terms can a president serve?
Two (2)

49. Who was Martin Luther King, Jr.?
A civil rights leader

50. Who is the head of your local government?
Different answers for every local government. For

the city of San Jose, California the answer is Mayor Ron Gonzales

51. According to the Constitution, a person must meet certain requirements in order to be eligible to become president. Name one of these requirements.
- Must be a natural born citizen of the United States
- Must be at least 35 years old by the time he/she will serve
- Must have lived in the United States for at least 14 years

52. Why are there 100 senators in the United States Senate?
Two (2) from each state

53. Who selects the Supreme Court justices?
Appointed by the president

54. How many Supreme Court justices are there?
Nine (9)

55. Why did the Pilgrims come to America?
For religious freedom

56. What is the head executive of a state government called?
Governor

57. What is the head executive of a city government called?
Mayor

58. What holiday was celebrated for the first time by the American colonists?
Thanksgiving

59. Who was the main writer of the Declaration of Independence?
   Thomas Jefferson

60. When was the Declaration of Independence adopted?
   July 4, 1776

61. What is the basic belief of the Declaration of Independence?
   That all men are created equal

62. What is the national anthem of the United States?
   The Star-Spangled Banner

63. Who wrote the Star-Spangled Banner?
   Francis Scott Key

64. Where does freedom of speech come from?
   The Bill of Rights

65. What is the minimum voting age in the United States?
   Eighteen (18)

66. Who signs bills into law?
   The president

67. What is the highest court in the United States?
   The Supreme Court

68. Who was the president during the Civil War?
   Abraham Lincoln

69. What did the Emancipation Proclamation do?
   Freed many slaves

70. What special group advises the president?
   The Cabinet

71. Which president is called the "Father of our Country?"
George Washington

72. What immigration and Naturalization Service form is used to apply to become a naturalized citizen?
Form N-400,"Application to file petition for Naturalization"

73. Who helped the Pilgrims in America?
The American Indians (Native Americans)

74. What is the name of the ship that brought the Pilgrims to America?
The Mayflower

75. What were the 13 original states of the United States called?
Colonies

76. Name 3 rights or freedoms guaranteed by the Bill of Rights.

- The right of freedom of speech, press, religion, peaceable assembly, and requesting change of government
- The right to bear arms (the right to have weapons or own a gun, though subject to certain regulations)
- The government may not quarter, or house, soldiers in the people's homes during peacetime without the people's consent
- The government many not search or take a person's property without a warrant
- A person may not be tried twice for the same crime and does not have to testify against him/herself

- A person charged with a crime still has some rights, such as the right to trial and to have a lawyer
- The right to trial by jury
- Protects people against excessive or unreasonable fines or cruel and unusual punishment
- The people have rights other than those mentioned in the Constitution. Any power not given to the federal government by the Constitution is a power of either the state or the people

77. Who has the power to declare war?
The Congress

78. What kind of government does the United States have?
Republican (as in "a republic": a type of government)

79. Which president freed the slaves?
Abraham Lincoln

80. In what year was the Constitution written?
1787

81. What are the first 10 amendments to the Constitution called?
The Bill of Rights

82. Name one purpose of the United Nations.
For countries to discuss and try to resolve world problems; to provide economic aid to many countries

83. Where does Congress meet?
In the Capitol in Washington, D.C.

84. Whose rights are guaranteed by the Constitution and the Bill of Rights?
Everyone (citizens and non-citizens living in the U.S.)

85. What is the introduction to the Constitution called?
The Preamble

86. Name one benefit of being a citizen of the United States.
- Obtain federal jobs
- Travel with a U.S. passport
- Petition for close relatives to come to the U.S. to live

87. What is the most important right granted to U.S. citizens?
The right to vote

88. What is the United States Capitol?
The place where Congress meets

89. What is the White House?
The president's official home

90. Where is the White House located?
Washington, D.C. (1600 Pennsylvania Avenue, NW)

91. What is the name of the president's official home?
The White House

92. Name one right guaranteed by the first amendment.
Freedom of speech, freedom of press, freedom of religion, freedom of peaceable assembly, and freedom of requesting change of the government

93. Who is the Commander in Chief of the U.S. military?
The president

94. Which president was the first Commander in Chief of the U.S. Military?
George Washington

95. In what month do we vote for the president?
    November

96. In what month is the new president inaugurated?
    January

97. How many times may a senator be re-elected?
    There is no limit

98. How many times may a congressman be re-elected?
    There is no limit

99. What are the 2 major political parties in the U.S. today?
    Democratic and Republican

100. How many states are there in the United States?
     Fifty (50)

101. Who said give me liberty or give me death?
     Patrick Henry

102. Name your state's two US Senators.
     Answers will depend on applicant's state of residence. For residents of the District of Columbia or of territories, such as Guam, the answer will be "N/A" because there aren't any.

103. Who is the Secretary of State now?
     Answer may depend on the year. As of 2007:
     A: Dr. Condoleezza Rice or "Condoleezza Rice," or "Dr. Rice."

104. What are two Cabinet-level positions?
     A: Secretary of Agriculture
     A: Secretary of Commerce
     A: Secretary of Defense
     A: Secretary of Education
     A: Secretary of Energy
     A: Secretary of Health and Human Services

A: Secretary of Homeland Security

A: Secretary of Housing and Urban Development

A: Secretary of Interior

A: Secretary of State

A: Secretary of Transportation

A: Secretary of Treasury

A: Secretary of Veterans' Affairs

A: Secretary of Labor

A: Attorney General

105. Under our Constitution, some powers belong to the states. What is <u>one</u> power of the states?

A: provide schooling and education

A: provide protection (police)

A: provide safety (fire departments)

A: give a driver's license

A: approve zoning and land use

106. What are <u>two</u> rights of everyone living in the United States?

A: freedom of expression

A: freedom of speech

A: freedom of assembly

A: freedom to petition the government

A: freedom of worship

A: the right to bear arms

107. There were 13 original states. Name <u>three</u>.

A: New Hampshire

A: Massachusetts

A: Rhode Island

A: Connecticut

A: New York

A: New Jersey

A: Pennsylvania

A: Delaware

A: Maryland

A: Virginia

A: North Carolina

A: South Carolina

A: Georgia

108. Name <u>one</u> American Indian tribe in the United States. [Adjudicators will be supplied with a complete list.]

A: Cherokee

A: Navajo

A: Sioux

A: Chippewa

A: Choctaw

A: Pueblo

A: Apache

A: Iroquois

A: Creek

A: Blackfeet

A: Seminole

A: Cheyenne

A: Arawak

A: Shawnee

A: Mohegan

A: Huron

A: Oneida

A: Lakota

A: Crow

A: Teton

A: Hopi

A: Inuit

109. Name one of the two longest rivers in the United States.

A: Missouri (River)
A: Mississippi (River)

110. What ocean is on the West Coast of the United States?

A: Pacific (Ocean)

111. Why do people go up the Empire State Building and then pay money to look at things on the ground via binoculars?

A: I have no idea!

Section 22) A Common Language:
English, Italian or Spanish?

Believe it or not English is not the official language of the United States. Many times the government has voted and introduced bills to make English the official language but for political reasons, it has narrowly been defeated.

However if you can speak English you will succeed, apart from a few TV and Radio stations, most broad cast in English. It's a touchy subject in some areas, early Italian and Polish immigrants soon learnt and spoke English. The high Spanish speaking population (this is the fastest growing population) often refuse to learn English, many of the children do speak English but the parents won't change. Therefore you will see many street signs in both English and Spanish.

When you phone a bank or utility company for example you will be asked to press 1 for English. Some of the 'Old School' Americans do not like this, but I can foresee no change. Infact if you travel to Miami you should have some basic Spanish speaking skills. You will find it almost impossible to order a cheese burger at MacDonald's in English. The official count is One in 7 people speak Spanish, that's over 43 million and its growing. If you are considering the move to the United States, you will most certainly need English speaking skills, but Spanish will help you and your family.

A British person feels that American is a foreign language. The Americans do not Hoover the carpets they vacuum them. They don't have dust bins, they have trash cans. In England the wood trim that fits around a room on the floor is called a skirting board, In the US it's a base board.

When it comes to cars the US and England have a complete different language:

UK	US
Bonnet	Hood
Boot	Trunk
Petrol	Gas
Wing	Fender
Windscreen	Windshield
You toot or beep your horn	You sound your horn
Indicators	Turning singles
Hazard warning lights	Blinkers
Spanner	Wrench
Wheel & Tyre	Rim & Tire
Motorway	Interstate
Dual Carriageway	Freeway

That's just cars; hundreds of other words are different:

Solicitor	Attorney
Car	Auto
Bathroom	Lavatory
Sweets/chocolate	Candy
Mobile phone	Cell Phone

Completion (property)	Closing
Autumn	Fall
Tap	Faucet
Walk	Hike
Plot of land	Lot
Timber	Lumber
Car Park	Parking Lot
Railway	Railroad
Property	Real Estate
Estate Agent	Realtor
Lavatory	Restroom
Pavement	Sidewalk
Cashier	Teller
Path	Trail
Flat	Condo or apartment
Rubbish	Trash
Garden	Yard
Gardening	Working in the yard
Give way	Yield
Post code	Zip Code
Mum	Mom
Taxi	Cab

If you noticed the difference to spelling the word Tyre/Tire there is lot more:

UK	US
Centre	Center
Colour	Color
Calibre	Caliber
Licence	License

Section 23) Working in the United States.

Working in the United States.

Many Americans work very hard and play hard too. The Americans have less vacation days than the workers in Europe. Most will work 40 hours minimum and it's not uncommon for people to hold 2 jobs. Many teachers are also Real Estate agents, many hairdressers, also wait on tables in the evenings. The United States also has the highest amount of small businesses per capita than any other country in the world.

Unlike Europe, if a person's business fails in America, It is just spoken of, they could not make a go of it and that's it. No stigma is attached; you are not seen as a failure. Many will go on and try again and after, sometimes two or three attempts before being successful. A majority of small business owners are one man bands, window cleaners, pool cleaners, locksmiths, car repair garages, they may have 1 or 2 employees later, but build up to this point. America is the franchise capital of the world. You have hundreds of franchises to choose. Companies such as Starbucks, Subway, Pizza Hut, KFC, MacDonald's, UPS/FedEx stores, Burger King, Marriott Hotels, Dunkin Donuts, Hilton Hotels, Holiday Inn Express, Gold's Gym, Dollar Rent a Car, Prudential Real Estate to Radio Shack. The choice is endless they all vary in initial outlay and all offer training and store build out to new owners. The Franchisors want the franchisees to be a success, so they will do everything they can to help you succeed. The bad news is that you have to pay a royalty, typically 4-7% of gross sales. But ask yourself would you buy your kids a meal at 'MacDonald's' or 'Joes Cheesy burger joint'. It's these small businesses that run the American economy.

Also unlike Europe approx 30% of Americans are paid no sick leave, that's nearly 30 million workers, plus the same amount have no health insurance. Plus American employers are not liable to pay redundancy money, or paid sick leave for a woman have a baby. In most States such as Florida you can almost hire and fire at will. You do NOT have to give a reason, if you do give a reason, then just use common sense; you are not required to give warnings or written warnings.

Vacation Pay

Again many States do not require an employer to give holiday pay, most pay on public holidays, such as July 4th (Independence Day) or Christmas day, but some employers will only pay this after a qualifying period of up to one year in some cases. The employees do have some rights, just not as good as Europe. It's illegal to discriminate against employees because of race, sex, national origin, age, pregnancy, marriage status, religion or weight. Some federal laws also protect employees against discrimination against the handicap and a BIG NO, NO is to discriminate against the sacred veterans. All ex service personnel in the United States are treated with the respect they deserve for their service for their country. Likewise a woman doing the same job as a man is to be paid the same wage, and job advertisements cannot discriminate against age or sex. You do not have to retire at 65 or 67 in the US. However an employer who wants to employ some young female models for a cat walk to show a new bra range for example can simply not hire a 75 year old overweight bald man with no teeth who applies for the job. *This is a grey area*!

Wages & Salary

The wage you are paid is normally the amount offered when you start the job and sign the contract, each State has its own laws regarding overtime rates for example. In the State of Florida if you work over 40 Hours anything over 40 hours must be paid at time and a half. In California, if you work 9.5 hours on the Monday and take the rest of the week off or just do a few hours a day for Tuesday- Friday, the fact that you did more than 8 hours on the Monday means you will get 1.5 hours at time and a half.

The minimum wage is set by the Fair Labor Standards Act. Again each state is different; every employer MUST post that particular States Minimum wage. Currently Florida is $7.45 per hour. Every work place should have this posted on a wall at the work place, along with labor requirements and details regarding WORKERS COMPENSATION. If you have 1 Spanish speaking member of staff, you must also have all the notices in Spanish and English.

Workers Compensation and the Legal system.

Workers Compensation is a requirement by law if an employer has at least 3 employees full or part time. It's an expensive insurance premium the employer must pay to cover his/her employees in the event of injury while at work. It was a great idea but the 'Slip and Fall' lawyers have abused it and actually advertise on Radio, TV and newspapers about making a claim against your employer, should you graze your knee or hurt your back. Many of the 'Slip & fall' Lawyers work on a no win no fee basis, any worker who gets fired or is just bored can simply say they had a fall or hurt their back.

Even if the case has NO merit and the employer is sure to win the case, Often the insurance company will settle out of court for a few thousand dollars. This is cheaper than hiring its own lawyer to go to court and fight the case. The end result is the employee gets approx 50% for the few thousand dollars, The 'Slip and Fall' lawyers get 50% of the fee for writing 2 or 3 letters and the poor employers insurance rates go through the roof. This is why so many small businesses in the United States stay small. When in America you will see and hear the 'Slip and Fall' lawyer advertisements, asking: Have you been bitten by a dog? Had an injury at work? Had a car accident? Injured yourself on someone's property, medical malpractice? Before you do anything call XXX XXX XXXX and we will give free and friendly advice, it won't cost you a cent.

In the United States there is 1 lawyer for every 575 people, Compare that to 1 lawyer for every 10,000 people in Japan, or 1 lawyer for every 6500 people in Great Britain. The United States legal system is based on federal law, this law is enacted by state legislatures. The freedom and rights of American people are 'written in stone' enshrined in the first ten amendments of the United States constitution, simply known as the 'Bill of rights'. This constitution was written in 1787 (you will probably get this question if you apply for citizenship) American law and the United States constitution apply to everyone in America, regardless of citizenship or legal status. Illegal immigrants also have the same legal rights as American citizens. Under the United States constitution every state has the power to establish its own system of criminal and civil laws. The end result is 50 different state legal systems. So never assume that the law is the same in every state. Some states allow brothels, marriage at age 14, same sex marriage, Guns concealed or otherwise, some have no income tax, no sales tax, and of course different employer laws.

The United States Judiciary is independent of the Federal government; it consists of the Supreme Court, the US court of appeals and the US district courts. The Supreme Court is the highest court in the United States; it consists of nine judges that are appointed for life by the President. (This how a President can leave his mark long after he has left office) The decision of the Supreme Court is final and legally binding.

On the federal level, there are several different groups, including the coast guard. Also the customs bureau will have its own law enforcement branch. There are also other federal law enforcement agencies, such as the federal bureau of Investigation. (FBI) that can claim a fair amount of jurisdiction wherever, in any State or county. The crime rate in the United States has been decreasing over the last 15 years.

Laws in the US are categorized:

Misdemeanors

A misdemeanor is an offence punishable by a relatively in severe penalty, such as a fine or short term in prison or a term of community service. In some jurisdictions, those who are convicted of a misdemeanor are known as misdemeanants. Depending on the jurisdiction, examples of misdemeanors may include: petty theft, prostitution, public intoxication, simple assault, jay walking, dropping litter, disorderly conduct, trespass, vandalism, and other similar crimes. A Misdemeanant may be issued with a summons.

Felony

The term felony is used in common law systems for very serious crimes, whereas misdemeanors are considered to be less serious offenses. This distinction is principally used in criminal law in the United States legal system, where the federal government generally considers a crime punishable by more than five days up to a year in prison to be a misdemeanor, while considering crimes punishable by greater than a year in prison to be felonies; crimes of five days or less in prison, or no prison at all, are considered infractions. An arrest will probably involve being searched and ALWAYS handcuffed with (unlike the UK) hands behind ones back. You will be advised of your constitutional rights, also known as Miranda rights. You will be asked if you wish to waive your rights. At the sheriff's office or police station you will be allowed to make a phone call. This should be to your embassy. You WILL BE photographed and this will be posted on the local website and often local newspapers, plus you WILL be put in a cell until your case comes before a judge. Normally the same or next day. You will get you day in court and a chance to speak, if you can't afford an attorney the state will provide one for you.

Section 24) Religion in the United States.

The United States has a tradition of religious tolerance. You will find every religious belief known to man represented somewhere in the United States, but the country is predominantly Catholic. This religion is growing due to the influx of Mexicans. Every resident of the United States has complete freedom of religion without hindrance from the local community or State. America is a country where the right to religious freedom and the separation of church and state are important yet violate issues. It seems logical that if a resident has the right to worship any religion he or she pleases, then no one faith should have more control over any other over government, however sometimes religion does play a role in politics. The conservative Christian movement has found a base with the Republican Party and the line between church and state seems a bit blurred. This despite the fact that it is enshrined in the First Amendment of the US constitution. In most parts of the world religion has seen a decline since the Second World War. However the United States has remained very religious, probably one of the World's most deeply religious nations. You will hear the reference many times, God bless America, In God we trust and one nation under God. It is estimated that over 90 % of Americans believe in God. In the UK & Canada it is said that only 60% believe in God.

One of the fastest growing religions is Mormonism. Also known as the Church of Jesus Christ of Latter-day, it is based in Salt Lake City. Its numbers have grown by over 200% since the 1970's and across the world its numbers have grown by nearly 350%. As everything in the United States, The Mormon church is also a thriving business worth an estimated 38 billion dollars. Small change compared to the

Catholic Church in the United States. The Catholic Church is the largest land owner in New York City and the wealthiest church in the world. God is big business in America; TV evangelists are some of the highest paid presenters in the country. California is the birth place of many of the world's strangest religions (I am not mocking any religion, when I say strange, maybe I should say unusual) including 'The Moonies' 'The Rajneeshies' 'Hare Krishna' 'Scientology' and Transcendental Meditation.

In many towns and cities churches and religious meeting places out numbers bars by as many as 5-1. On a Sunday the streets are just as busy as week days with town's folk going to church. But the churches often offer more than just prayers and hymns, many have live music at worship, the gospel choirs have a huge following, many also offer sports and schooling.

<u>Section 25)</u> Education and School System.

This will be one of the biggest surprises you will have when you take your children to a school. The children are concerned about grades and work hard on keeping them. The majority of children want to graduate and know what grades they need to graduate, Most stay on until they are 18 and complete high school and go onto a college or university. American schools have the lowest level of bulling that of any other western country. Bullying is simply not tolerated at any level, even a 1st grader age 6 will be suspended if he or she dares to call a child wearing glasses four eyes or frog eyes.

Many schools will have a police officer present and when the school is closing will have a high police presence. After school activities such as football, baseball or basketball will also have a police presence; it gives security and peace of mind.

Kindergarten (this is German for Children's Garden) ages 2-5 Children are taught to develop basic skills through creative play and social interaction. In most states kindergarten is part of the pre-school system. The maximum 13 years of education covers education from age 5-18, divided into grades. If a child or Student fails some of the courses he or she must repeat a grade, although this is rare. However you can expect your children to struggle with history if they enter the school system after grade 4. But this is just 1 subject and some allowances can be made for immigrants.

1st Grade   Children aged 6 in Elementary or Primary school

2nd Grade   Children aged 7 in Elementary or Primary school

3rd Grade	Children aged 8 in Elementary or Primary school
4th Grade	Children aged 9 in Elementary or Primary school
5th Grade	Children aged 10 in Elementary or Primary school
6th Grade	Children aged 11 in Elementary or Primary school
7th Grade	Children aged 12 in Junior High or Middle school
8th Grade	Children aged 13 in Junior High or Middle school

3rd Grade — Children aged 8 in Elementary or Primary school

4th Grade — Children aged 9 in Elementary or Primary school

5th Grade — Children aged 10 in Elementary or Primary school

6th Grade — Children aged 11 in Elementary or Primary school

7th Grade — Children aged 12 in Junior High or Middle school

8th Grade — Children aged 13 in Junior High or Middle school

9th Grade — Children aged 14 in Junior High or Middle school
Freshman

10th Grade — Students aged 15 in Senior High or High school
Sophomore

11th Grade — Students aged 16 in Senior High or High school
Junior

12th Grade — Students aged 17 in Senior High or High school
Senior

To register your child at a school you MUST live in that Zip code. You can check the schools you want your children to attend and buy or rent a home in that school's catchment area. These areas can be found either on- line or just ask the school. You will need to provide proof of residency, a utility bill, rent or mortgage payment statement. Most schools prefer children / students to start at the beginning of a new school term or as it is called in the States, a semester, however this is not necessary. You will also need to provide birth certificate and most important medical history. Your child will NOT be accepted until he or she has had all the required immunizations or Shots as it is called here. These will include polio, Diphtheria, Tetanus, whooping cough, measles, mumps, and sometimes Tuberculin screening.

Many schools will have a part time or full time nurse and the staff are trained with first aid.

School Buses.

Many districts provide transport via a school bus system and depending on distance from school it's normally free. The yellow school buses run on a strict timetable and system, the drivers are not allowed out of their seats and will stop the bus and open the doors at every level crossing (Cross a railroad track) this is for safety reasons.

School hours and Terms.

This will vary from school to school; the term generally runs from the end of August to May (9 months) it is divided into terms, quarters, and semesters. If you wish to take your children out of school you should get permission from the principal and it's not often given unless it is for doctors or dentist. The hours at US schools vary from state to state. Some will start at 7am and finish at 1pm others may start as late as 9.30am and of course finish much later.

The summer recess is a long break in America for the children and students, however many American children from ages 10-17 attend summer camps. These are very well organized and safe. Some 15 million children attend a summer camp every year. Some are at the local church or karate center. Many are miles away even in other states, they spend typically 1-4 weeks at camp, the activities are endless. Traditional summer camps with hiking, swimming, climbing, fishing, and boating are most popular, but in more recent years they now have summer camps for special activities for whatever your child has an interest in.

Music camps are becoming popular where a child with a talent for any instrument can go to camp and become part of a band, group. Singing, dancing and composing, Sports camps that specialize in soccer, baseball, basket ball, American football, swimming, athletics, gymnastics, martial arts and cycling. There are now camps in Hollywood on film making and at NASA for would be or hopeful astronauts. Along with military camps. The summer camps give the children a chance to make new friends, learn to do things for themselves and gives them a break from mom and dad. (Yes in America you will be a mom not a mum) the summer camps are not free and can be expensive from $275 per week-$600+ but the children go back year after year and enjoy it.

School Security

Most middle and high schools provide students with lockers where they can store their books and gym clothing etc. A majority of schools also provide cycle racks for those who cycle to school. The high schools provide students with a parking lot (car park) for those 16 and up who drive themselves to school. *See Motoring.* However the school does have strict rules on students who drive themselves and friends to school. They must first take proof of insurance, driver's license and title of automobile. They will then be given a student pass, normally a sticker for the windshield and a parking place number. They can only park in this spot. They are also not allowed to return to the vehicle until school is finished and not allowed to remove the car at lunch time.

The Police or sheriff dept will have an office in most schools and encourage talks with the law enforcement agencies regarding safety and drug use. In some inner city schools metal detectors are at the entrance to prevent students taking weapons to school. In high crime areas school bags are banned from classes, the students must keep all books in the lockers and just carry the books needed for that particular lesson. This may sound a bit scary, but it's all done to protect your child.

At some schools with children as young as 12 issue free condoms, this can be done with or without parent's knowledge.

Along with sex education at age 10, this is a hot topic as some parents, do not want their children to know about sex, sex education, and contraception or be able to have access to condoms. I fail to see the argument, I am sure if a some parents found out a week later that their daughter had had sex, I am sure it would give them a little piece of mind if they knew it was with a boy who had been given sex education and free condoms, rather than a boy who knows nothing about sex education and is unable to get his hands on a condom. The community programs see it as a way of prevention of AIDS and unwanted pregnancies.

Examinations, Grades and level of Education.

I expect this section to be read over and over by parents who ask. How does the education compare to England, Canada, Australia, Europe or where ever you are from?

The simple answer is: *It's the same!*

When your child first enrolls in a public school a folder is opened. (Now it is an electric file) The folder/file will follow them throughout the school years. The grades they collect are continuous; Students are marked on each paper, exam and courses taken on every subject throughout the school life of the student.

The grades give a point for a total accumulation to provide details of whether or not they have passed those years courses.

Grade	Points	
A	4	Excellent or Superior
B	3	Good or above average
C	2	Average
D	1	Below Average or Poor minimum passing grade (60-69)
F	0	Fail (0-68) = 0.00

The grades can also be A+ or A- for example; they still carry the same point basis.

What does the point mean? To graduate high school a student must collect 22-28 points depending on subjects taken. Plenty of A's help, if your child fails a subject the schools do offer a summer class just for those particular subjects. It helps students catch up and act as a deterrent to slacking.

Percentage ranges may vary from one school to another. In some schools like those in Virginia Beach public schools use the 7-point grade system where the grades are given as follows: 100-94A, 93-86B, 85-78C, 77-70D, and 69 and below is failing, (E) In some schools, these ranges may even vary from one class to another. Many schools add .5 to the value of an AP class if a student takes the AP test (thus, an A would be a 4.5, a B would be a 3.5, etc). Also in California and many other states, taking the AP test adds a full point to a grade.

Whether the failing grade is F or E typically depends on time and geography. Some states, but not many, have tended to favor E since World War II while the majority of the country tends to use F. Ultimately, the grade F traces to the days of two-point grading as Pass (P) and Fail (F).

Chromatic variants (+ and −) are often used. In hypo modal grading on a 100 point scale, the prime letter grade is assigned a value centered on the one's digit 5, the + grade is assigned the top values of near the one's digit 9 and the − grade is assigned the bottom values near 0. Thus, 80 to 83 is B−, 84 to 86 is B, and 87 to 89 is B+. In straight modal grading on a 4.0 decimal scale, the prime number is the prime letter grade. The + range of the grade begins at X.333 (repeating), rounded to X.30, above the prime number. The − range of the grade begins at X.666 (repeating), rounded up to X.70, below the prime number. Thus, B = 3.0, B+ = 3.3, and B− = 2.7. However, the A range is often treated as a special case. In most American schools, a 4.00 is regarded as perfect and the highest GPA one can achieve. Thus, an A, being the prime grade, already achieves the mark of a 4.00; for the A+ mark, most schools assign it a value of 4.00, equivalent to the A mark, so as to not deviate from the standard 4.00 GPA system. The A+ mark, then, becomes a mark of distinction that has no impact on the student's GPA. A few schools do assign grade values of 4.33, however.

Class	Credits	Grade	Grade Points
Speech 101	3	A	$3 \times 4.0 = 12.0$
Biology 102	4	B+	$4 \times 3.3 = 13.2$
History 103	3	B−	$3 \times 2.7 = 8.1$
Physical Education 104	1	C	$1 \times 2.0 = 2.0$

Total Credits: 11

Total Grade Points: 35.3

Grade Point Average: 35.3 / 11 = 3.209 or slightly above B average

In a standards-based grading system, a performance standard is set by a committee based on ranking anchor papers and grading rubrics which demonstrate performance which is below, meeting, or exceeding the "Standard". The standard is intended to be a high, world class level of performance which must be met by every student, regardless of ability or class, although they are actually set by a committee with no reference to any other national standard. Levels are generally assigned numbers between zero and four. Writing papers may be graded separately on content (ideas) and conventions (spelling and grammar). Since grading is not based on a curve distribution, it is entirely possible to achieve a grading distribution where "all children succeed" and meet the standard. While such grading is generally used only for assessments, they have been proposed for alignment with classroom grading. However, in practice grading can be much more severe than the traditional letter grades rather than more generous. Even after ten years, states like Washington continue to grade over half of students as "below standard" on the state mathematics assessment.

The marks given depend on a range of criteria; this includes a student's performance in tests given at regular intervals during the school year, participation in class discussions, completion of homework assignments and independent projects. Your child will receive a report card twice a year some schools four times a year, which shows their grades in each subject they're studying. Commercially prepared tests are also given in many areas at all levels to assess students and schools achievements.

Elementary school curriculum varies with the educational aims of individual schools and local communities. Promotion from 1st Grade to the next is based on a student's achievements of specified skills, although a child is required to repeat a year in exceptional circumstances only. They will contact the parents well before the end of the school year and discuss ways to help the student pass the grades required. The elementary school will provide instruction in the funder mental sill of reading, writing and math's. Also PE (Physical Education) music, crafts, science, art, geography and not forgetting the very important history. Homework is a requirement of up to an hour per day in elementary school.

The file the student collects throughout his/her school life is collected and copies of this are submitted to the college. The acceptance of a student at a University or college is also based on this file. Therefore it is very important that the child gets good grades throughout his/her school life. Although the University or college will also require the student to take an aptitude test during the last two years of high school. These are set by independent institutions. The college of University will also require the student to take Achievement Tests. These tests are multiple choices and are not normally based directly on school work, but are designed to measure aptitude, verbal and mathematical skills. The most common test used are by the ACT (American College Testing) this is recognized by accredited universities to evaluate students.

If you have a ten year old child at a western school he or she will attend an elementary school and no doubt be a 5th Grader depending on birth date. He / she will be able to read and write and do mathematics. The first day at the American school will be like attending any new school; the same problems of getting lost and making new friends exist. However your child will have an advantage over his/her fellow students. They will have a different accent, children will want to hear them talk and soon make friends. Once this is established the rest becomes easy. The American public school is not advanced or behind from any other country, despite what you may hear. The American society does have a strong belief in education and your child will have without a doubt far more opportunities in America, more than any other country in the world. *No Child Left Behind* is a speech politicians often use.

Private Schools

You have your reasons: Maybe your child has special needs that you feel the public school system cannot provide. Perhaps you're less than satisfied with the academic achievements or the safety records of the public schools where you live. Perhaps you attended private school as a child and you want your children to enjoy the same experience. In America there are numerous private schools, serving a multitude of educational needs.

No matter what the reasons are that you've decided to enroll your child into private school the fact remains that deciding which school to send your child to is a tough decision. With so many schools from which to choose, the matter of selecting a school is not simple by any standards. Several aspects of school and child must be considered before arriving to a final decision. Approx 10% of American are taught in private school for a variety of reasons. These schools include single-sex schools, school sponsored by religious groups, schools for children with physical or learning disabilities and schools for gifted children be that academic or sports. When you start to weigh your options, you'll come across several practical constraints. You may want to find a school close to your workplace or your home. If you have more than one child, you may want them to attend the same school.

You will need to consider the following:

- How far must the child travel back and forth to school?

- Will there be a need for transportation or does the school provide transportation?

- Is there a need for before- or after-school care?

- Does your child have any physical, emotional, linguistic or learning needs that require special attention?

- What about costs? How much does the school cost? What is your budget for private school? If the school is too far for a daily commute, does it provide boarding?

- On that note, are you looking for a boarding school or must the school is within daily driving range?

- Must you have certain components in place at a private school before you'll consider it? For example, are you looking for a military school? Do you want religion to be a part of your child's education? Do you want a school where boys and girls are kept separate?

- Is college preparation a priority? Some parents look for science curriculum and some want a top music program.

- Are modern school facilities important to you?

- Does your child need small school environment, or a large school?

- Do you want a school with several grade levels, such as K-12, where your child can remain for several years?

- Consider the instructional model. Do you want a traditional, back-to-basics program or an alternative approach to learning?

- Do you want a school where parents are expected to be involved with activities and decisions?

- How does the school communicate with parents?

- What music and art programs are important to you?

- Are sports important? Which ones?

- . What clubs would your child like to attend at school?

- Read the underlying philosophy of the school; ask about the beliefs that guide the school's program and teaching approaches.

- Check the services available at the school such as counselors, an on-site nurse, librarian, and a secretary.

- Look at the structure of the school year. Is it a year-round school or a more traditional school calendar?

- What is the background and qualification of the teachers?

- Examine the school discipline policy to see if the rules seem fair and consequences seem appropriate.

- Look at the school curriculum. Find out the homework and grading policies.

- Find out about the facility in case of an emergency. How are parents notified in case of an emergency? What is the school's policy on guns, knives, and other hazardous items, towards bullying etc.?

• Does the school have any special program and policies related to parent involvement? What type of relationship does the school have with local businesses and community groups for guest speakers, financial support etc.? This relationship can contribute to the quality of the school and the support that it enjoys in the community.

• Is this school accredited? If so, how?

• What professional development opportunities do teachers have? In what ways do teachers collaborate?

• What are some of the school's greatest accomplishments? What are some of the biggest challenges this school faces?

• How are students graded?

• What is the class-size? Smaller class-size is better, especially in the primary grades. Is the library/media center well equipped and organized? Can children regularly check out books and use the center's resources?

• What is their teaching methodology? Do teachers work by themselves with students in small groups or do they work in teams to teach larger groups.

• How does this school encourage and monitor students' progress toward meeting academic standards? How does this school use technology to support teaching and learning?

• How does this school support students with academic, social or emotional difficulties?

• What is this school's policy for students who speak English as a second language? What strategies do they use to teach students who are not fluent in English? If your child does not speak English, How to they help?

Religious instruction is not permitted in State or public schools. Because of this many private schools are based on religious principles. The range is never ending and still growing as new religions pop up. There are some famous Catholic convent schools, Jewish schools, Baptist, Islamic, and Mormon schools. The list is never ending. Church organized or run schools are usually referred to collectively as 'Parochial' schools. It is said that some schools, such as Catholic schools are set up in attempt to create all-white schools, and Baptist as all-black schools. I will make no comment or remark on the subject.

After you've visited the private schools, you've hopefully gathered all the information you need to make a decision about which school to enroll your child in. After you've filtered out any schools that didn't meet your practical requirements, you should be left with a short-list of schools which you researched. Careful research should have ranked these schools at which point you'd want to look at the extracurricular activities as well as scheduled campus visits.

Now you should prioritize the schools that you want your child to attend and then apply to as many as you feel you need to in order to safely get your child into at least one of them for the following year. Many parents will apply to more than one private school so that they can reserve a spot at that school in case they should want to go. It doesn't hurt to apply to your top three choices with the plan that if your first two don't accept you or run out of space, you can always enroll your children into your third school. However, in case of private schools, one has to plan ahead because most private schools make admission decisions for the following school year by January of the current year. The most important advice you'll ever hear is to start early. Start your search early, plan your visits early, and put in your applications early. Each school has its own requirements, and some documentation (independent testing, for example) may take a while to gather. Pay attention to admission requirements and deadlines.

Be sure to get references from any school you are seriously considering. Some of your best information will come from parents with students already enrolled at the school. What do they see as strengths and concerns at the school and in the community? So get you applications in as far in advance as possible, OK it may not be that easy if you are waiting for your visa, but there is nothing to stop you applying before your visa is accepted. It's usually easier to be accepted at a school to the first grade than to get a child into a later grade, where entry is limited. Some schools will facilitate entry for some foreign children. They consider it an advantage to have children or students from different countries.

An important step for you to take is to be fully aware of withdrawal conditions. You cannot simply remove your child. You will have signed a contract with the school; they would have made a place available. This is very important as it could be costly, it maybe that the school is too advanced for your child's capabilities. You can successfully sail through selecting the best school, if you do your own homework early! Prioritize your needs. Remember you must do this first or otherwise you'll have a tough time picking one private school over another. Learn as much as you can about your candidate private schools. As long as you've prioritized your needs, you should be able to rank the candidate private schools. There's nothing like seeing a school in person. Informative visits will definitely help you get a good feel for the school's milieu, both academic and when the kids are out of class. The last thing we can leave you with is to start early! Give yourself plenty of time so that you don't end up letting full enrollments make your private school selection for you.

Private School Fees

Fees vary from school to school depending on the school. Some Church schools are actually free to the parishioners, while others treat as a business, but can offer more. Most fees will vary according to a variety of factors including the age of the students, the reputation and quality of the school and its location. You can typically expect annual fees to start at $500 - $18,000. Boarding schools can cost up to $35,000. You can try for a scholarship and most private schools do offer these, but to will have an uphill climb with this as you are an immigrant and until you have some years in the school system in the United States, it's almost unheard of for an immigrant to get a grant over an American citizen.

Some parents would never consider sending their children to a public school, and they have their reasons. Other parents would never consider a private school, and they also have their reasons. If you fall into one of these camps and are completely satisfied with the choices you've made, congratulations. If you're still undecided, however, join the club!

<u>Section 26)</u> Driving in America.

The American made Hummer *circa 2007*

Typical American Interstate, San Diego, California *Circa 2008*

America has a love affair with the automobile. Many Europeans are shocked by the fact that Americans just don't walk anywhere. I live in a small street, 150 yards in length; my neighbor will drive to the end and back to buy a newspaper from a newspaper vending machine. The street is flat and its Sunny Florida, nevertheless he drives.

The United States is the drive in or drive through capital of the world, we have drive in Movies, Burgers (all the makes), Kentucky Fried Chicken, Taco Bell, Pizza, Starbucks, Dunkin Do nuts, Most Pharmacies, Most Banks, ATM machines, Goodwill charity drop off, Ice cream bars, Chinese food, DVD rental, Dry cleaners, clinics, Religious services and in Las Vegas the ultimate with drive through weddings. Every Americans dream is to own a car in some states at age 15 they can take a driving test and drive a car. Many high schools teach driving to the students and by participating in the schemes students or their parents will receive a discount from the insurance companies.

There are over 225 million vehicles on American roads; the population of America is just over 300 million. The United States has the highest ration of vehicles to population. Plus the registered number of vehicles is more than the recorded registered drivers, as many people in America own more than one vehicle.

Depending on where you are coming from, in America they drive on the left. The same side as the majority of Europe,

Japan, South America. The American and many Europeans will often say that the 'Brits' drive on the wrong side of the road. So why do the countries drive on different sides of the road? It cost's motor manufactures a fortune. In the late 1700s, however, teamsters in France and the United States began hauling farm products in big wagons pulled by several pairs of horses. These wagons had no driver's seat; instead the driver sat on the left rear horse, so he could keep his right arm free to lash the team. Since he was sitting on the left, he naturally wanted everybody to pass on the left so he could look down and make sure he kept clear of the oncoming wagon's wheels. Therefore he kept to the right side of the road.

In addition, the French Revolution of 1789 gave a huge impetus to right-hand travel in Europe. The fact is, before the Revolution, the aristocracy travelled on the left of the road, forcing the peasantry over to the right, but after the storming of the Bastille and the subsequent events, aristocrats preferred to keep a low profile and joined the peasants on the right. An official keep-right rule was introduced in Paris in 1794, more or less parallel to Denmark, where driving on the right had been made compulsory in 1793

Napoleon required the countries he conquered to conform to French practice. In Finland for another 50 years they drove and travelled on the left. It wasn't until 1858 that an Imperial Russian decree made Finland swap sides. Most British colonies drive on the same side as Britain (left) India, Australia although not Egypt as it has previously been conquered by Napoleon. Up till the 1930s Spain lacked national traffic regulations. Some parts of the country drove on the right (e.g. Barcelona) and other parts drove on the left (e.g. Madrid). On the 1st of October 1924 Madrid switched to driving on the right. China changed to the right in 1946.

- Did the United States ever drive on the left?

- Yes. It seems almost certain that in the early years of English colonization of North America, English driving customs were followed and the colonies drove on the left, gradually changing to right-hand driving after independence. Kincaid quotes an English author writing in 1806 as saying, "in some parts of the United States, it is a custom among the people to drive on the right side of the road," implying that in other parts, people still drove on the left. However, Kincaid is not convinced that left-hand driving was ever widespread in the American colonies. That's because the colonists were not exclusively English (for example, the Dutch settlers of New Amsterdam, which later became New York, would have been accustomed to driving on the right), and says that the first vehicles used by the colonists were carts. Wagons like the stagecoach (best driven on the left) were not introduced until much later -- too late to change the established practice.

- If you take to the open road you can drive for miles without seeing another vehicle (or anyone), and if you try to drive in New York City, the average speed is 17 miles per hour. The huge advantage to driving in America is that the road's are on a grid like system, Think of a box table and that is how the roads in most towns and cities are laid out. It's very easy to find your way around, as most streets have numbers, such as 42nd street, the next block is 43rd street and so on. Cross streets are often called the same with east or west added. So if you are looking for 42nd Street West, just drive along 42nd Street until you see 42nd Street west. It really is very easy. Some of the cities are terrible in Rush hours, just like all major cities throughout the world. Try and avoid rush hours, which can be a complete nightmare.

Times will vary according to the city, but are usually between 7-9.00 am, and from 4-6.30pm. Many cities experience heavy traffic jams on Fridays, when the mad weekend rush starts, and again on Sundays when they return.

• If you do drive in the USA, remember that each of the 50 states has its own set of traffic laws and regulations. Fortunately, most of the laws are the same, but some states have slightly different rules. When you rent a car, you should ask the agent if there are any special driving rules in that state. When driving in multiple states, check a tour book for any special driving rules in each state.

• I travelled to the United States for many years and always drove but I did not know the following, I was lucky and had no problems, but you may not be.

• When a school bus stops and has its lights flashing, you must STOP. Even if you are on the other side of the road. (Unless there is a median or center island splitting the roads) All buses and fuel tankers will stop at train (level crossings) crossings. You must come to a complete stop at a stop sign. If you are turning right and the traffic signal is red, you are allowed to treat it as a stop sign and if it is clear and no signage to say otherwise, you are allowed to pull out and turn right. If you don't turn right at the red light, angry local drivers behind you will let you know.

• Speed limits in America vary by state. Be sure to check for information relating to your specific destinations. In the USA toll roads are referred to as Turnpikes.

• As you enter a turnpike you are sometimes issued a ticket, which may record the time. Be aware that if you reach the exit of the Turnpike at a time that indicates you have been breaking the speed limit, you will get a ticket! The tolls are based on the distance you drive.

- To obtain details of toll roads across the US, you will need to contact local transport representatives.

- Drive on the right. In general the roads in the USA are in good condition, but bear in mind the scale of the country is reflected in the long, straight roads you are likely to encounter when travelling across states. Ensure you take breaks to keep your concentration fresh.

- American Automobile Association Benefits: If you are a member of a motor club in your native country you may also receive some of the benefits that the American equivalent, The American Automobile Association (AAA, commonly called the "Triple A") offers. Take your membership card as proof.

- Triple A has offices in every city across the US and most of the larger towns. The benefits associated with Triple A include provision of free maps and tourist guides and discounts in some hotels.

- If you are not a member of any motor club you can buy membership to Triple A at any office in the US. However for a short trip and with a rental car this will not be required. The majority of hire cars will have cover from AAA.

- The US highway system: In the US the long stretches of roads across the states are called Interstate Highways. These highways are sometimes subject to tolls (these roads are called Turnpikes). All of the major Interstate Highways running north-south have odd numbers, on the Pacific coast they are ordered 1-5 and on the Atlantic coast are ordered 1-95. All east-west Interstates are evenly numbered. Those near the Mexican border begin either 1-8 or 1-10, but as you get closer to Canada they begin 1-94.

- Travelling with children: Children are made to feel very welcome in the majority of US tourist attractions, and there are certainly a lot on offer to choose from. It is worth checking out the government tourism website for the state(s) you are visiting as they usually list the attractions you will find on your travels. For further information and links to tourism sites, see our individual state listings.

- When travelling with your family in the US, driving yourselves does have many benefits if you are confident as a driver and plan ahead. Ensure that you familiarize yourself with the routes you are likely to take and the US rules of the road well in advance of your visit. Some inner city areas should be avoided as tourists are targeted by local criminals, this problem has been well publicized in the past and local organizations will be able to help you establish the places to avoid. Before you set off on a trip out in the car, plan your stop off points and take with you drinks, snacks, and diversions to keep children entertained whilst you are concentrating on driving. As you would in your own country, it is advisable to avoid big cities at rush hour as this is when driving can be most difficult. Please note in most states it is ILLEGAL to travel with a young child under 9 without them being in a child seat. You will get a ticket and can be placed in jail for child abuse. It is also law in many states for adults to wear a seat belt.

- <u>Driving license:</u>

- In the U.S.A you are not required to carry an International Driving Permit (IDP) if you hold a valid driving license, but often you are required to have held your license for a minimum of one year and a foreign driving license is normally only valid for a year. Every state is different here, so please find out what your state law is. For example in Florida you are only allowed to drive on a foreign passport for 30 days. After this period you have to take the driving test.

- In the U.S.A and Canada driving license's include the drivers photograph, so if you are from a country where this is not the case it is wise to also carry your passport to avoid any unnecessary complications or delays should you have to produce it. If you are from the U.K. remember to take both parts of your driving license (photo card and paper license with the further details).

- <u>Driving in the rain or Fog:</u>

- In most US states you are required to use headlights when it is raining or poor visibility.

- <u>California Driving</u>

- Most of California is nearly inaccessible without a car. California has almost no convenient or safe public transport. If you're a tourist taking a vacation or holiday in California, you'll soon discover that, except for small parts of the San Francisco Bay Area, where public transport can be fairly convenient and safe (and sometimes the best way to get around); most tourist areas or naturally-beautiful places are only realistically accessible by car or crowded tourist bus. Most people who fly into California, whether for business or for vacation, will rent a car when they get here, there's simply no cheaper or more convenient and safe way to get to and from the airport and you're other destinations. In nearly every part of the state, it is always quicker and more convenient, and safer to take a car than to use public transport, assuming public transport exists there at all. Similarly, if you've just moved to California (or are thinking of doing this), you're almost certainly going to need a car to get to work, do the shopping, and generally survive.

- <u>New York City Driving.</u>

- Don't drive drunk! You shouldn't do this anywhere, but especially not in New York. With the new laws, your car can be seized by the police. No right turns on red in NYC! In every other city in the United States you are allowed to make a right turn on a red light after a full stop. However, in

New York City this is illegal, unless otherwise noted by a traffic sign. Do not contribute to grid-lock! Enter an intersection only if you're sure you can make it through! In some locations gridlock is not only obnoxious, but it's illegal and subject to fine. Even more compelling, with the proliferation of handguns and lethal weapons, who knows when a crazy driver will take a few shots at you for blocking his/her way. Check the red signs with the street cleaning symbol to make sure you don't have to move your car the next day. This is NYC's attempt to give the street sweepers a chance to clean the streets. Leave nothing valuable showing in the driver's cab. When placing belongings into the trunk, do so before finding a parking spot. Many car burglars hide and watch people place valuables into the trunk then strike after the driver has left. If something is valuable to you, carry it with you! Some people leave nice signs informing robbers that there's nothing valuable inside the car. Some areas (ie. Holland Tunnel entrance) forbid the sounding of the car horn, with a fine of $100 for violators. This is usually found in areas with a large number of residences. If someone approaches your car at a stop light to either ask for money, wash your windows or sell you something, try to ignore them. If you do, for some reason, feel inclined to give the person money, remove it very discretely from your pocket. Then open the window a crack and slide the money through it. An open window in a car makes you a very vulnerable target.

- ### Florida

- You can turn right on Red, unless stated. You can do a 'U' turn in most places unless it says No 'U' turns. Florida does have its 'Snowbird' season. Normally the end of October to the end of April. The 'Snowbirds' are normally retirees who live in the northern States, NY, MI, CT, WA, NJ, OH or even Canada. These people are sometimes very elderly. Many are still driving at over 90 years of age, However they still drive the huge cars, it's very common place to a huge Buick or Cadillac driving very slow and crossing from lane to lane, without giving signals. At first glance you will assume the car is driving it' self as you can see no driver. But if you look close: just at steering wheel level you will see a mop of white or grey hair. This is a little old lady who peers through the steering wheel. Generally they are very safe drivers and they are in no hurry, they are retired and have plenty of time. The problem is with the local people who are trying to get about to work and go about their business, it can be very frustrating. I have seen some bumper stickers on some of Florida's younger generation saying: *"When I get old I am going to Move north and Drive Slow"* The worst time is 4.30pm-7.00pm. Many of the Dinners and restaurants will offer discounts to seniors who arrive early, It's called the 'Early Bird Special" Then the roads are very busy with our seniors off to dinner with friends. The simple way to avoid trouble is to have patients. Many of these seniors fought in the war for us, and now just want a quite life and to be able to spend six months a year in paradise: Florida.

• Florida's "Move Over Act," passed in 2002, requires drivers to move over to the next lane or slow down (at least 20 miles below the posted speed limit) while approaching emergency vehicles that are stopped on interstate or other highways.

• I can't cover all 50 states in one book, at the back of the book; I have included some websites that will help you. But again never assume that the motoring laws in one state are the same as in another state.

• Parking

• Before parking your car make sure it is in a designated area as otherwise you may be liable for the car being towed away. Do not park in front of a fire hydrant. You will find most of the cars are a lot larger than at home but to compensate for this the car parks have much bigger parking spaces.

- **Car Hire:**

- It is normally possible for foreign visitors to use their native driving license within the U.S.A. for a period of up to one year. Be aware that the minimum age permissible to rent a car is generally 21 years, and in some instances 25 years. Check with the rental company you plan to hire the car with if you are a younger or older driver (over 70 years) and be advised that there may be further charges related to your age.

- You will need a valid credit card for payment. If you are going to rent a car, it is wise to clarify the details and requirements prior to your departure to avoid any problems. If you are a member of an automobile association check and see if you are eligible to any discounts. It is worth finding out if there is a 'drop-off' charge made if you pick a car up in one location but take it back to another, although many car rental companies are doing away with this in a bid to become more competitive. Car rental companies can usually supply child car seats, check at the time of booking, this will usually incur an additional charge. If you are planning to purchase extra items such as a damage waiver or insurance, you should also comparison shop those rates.

- Make sure their mileage policy is favorable to you so you can avoid extra charges. Airport fees can be quite large so you might see if it is worth it to use an off-airport facility. However, if the off-airport company picks you up at the airport, you'll probably still have to pay some of the fee. Make your reservation as soon as you have decided on plans. Most Rental Car Companies increase their rates as reservations come in and their fleets become booked. Also, certain classes of cars will sell out and you may end up reserving and paying for a larger vehicle than you want. Being flexible about your travel plans can save you money. Rental Companies that focus on the business or replacement market customers often have great weekend specials. The best rates are found during the off season and at other times when the Rental Companies have extra cars sitting around.

- Book the smallest car that you will need and hope for a free upgrade. But, remember you may get stuck with that small car. Check into other size class vehicles. They may have extra cars in a certain class and be offering discounts for that size class. Use coupons, but read them carefully for exceptions. Most upgrade coupons are "based on availability", so if you have an upgrade coupon that you wish to use and also have a monetary discount coupon, bring them both. If they can't honor the upgrade, they may still give you the monetary discount.

- Can I rent a car seat?

- In many states it is illegal to travel with a child under the age of 8 without a child seat, although all states have different laws. Most car rental companies do carry child seats; however please book these in advance to avoid disappointment. The costs vary from company to company; Hertz was offering the child seats free of charge but promotions can start and end at will.

'Honest Harry's Truck Rental'. *Circa 1983*

Importing your Vehicle

Unless it's a very rare classic, why would you want to? The United States is the cheapest place in the world to buy a car. But it can be done, first make sure you are aware of current regulations. Taking a new car to the United States is a complete waste of time and money unless you really want a French car. (Citroen, Peugeot and Renault) most other makes are for sale in the U.S.

All vehicles entering the United States must meet the standards under the Motor Vehicle Safety Act of 1996. This was later revised in 1988. Also they must conform to the bumper standards of 1972. I can personally remember how I was disappointed when MG sports cars of Great Britain changed all new sports cars in 1973. To be allowed in the U.S market they removed the classic chrome bumpers and changed them to a pathetic looking black rubber version. This was just to be able to sell in the U.S. But they also sold this new type in the rest of the world. (OK, I got that off my chest). Your vehicle must also meet the clean air act of

1968. You have nothing to worry about there; most standards around the world are higher than in the U.S. The duty on foreign made vehicles new or used imported to the United States is set at 2.5% of the vehicles value and 3.4% on motorcycles.

It's a lot easier to export a vehicle from the United States and with the current value of the U.S Dollar it is a growing practice.

Vehicle Registration

The license plate is different in the States compared to Europe and Australia. Unlike Europe the license plate (Number plate) stays with the owner not the vehicle. The plate does not show a year or date of vehicle. Each State will have their own plates and laws. Did you know in Florida, Arizona and another 29 States you only have a license plate on the back of the car? Yet New York for example with has a plate on the front and back of the car. Each car will also have a small sticker (tag) this will have a date of expiration. When you apply for a new tag, it will expire on your birth month. Example: Elvis Presley born in January would have had a tag with number 01/77. If he was alive today it would be 01/2009. However company cars all have the date 06 or 08 month. If you have had a rental car it will have this month and of course the date. If you are caught by a Sheriff, Police officer or Highway patrol officer you will be fined for having an expired tag.

All cars in the United States have to be registered and must have a certificate of title. To register a vehicle in your name and address, you will need to go to a local DMV office (Department of Motor vehicles) of Tax office depending on what state you are in.

You will also need proof of ownership, your ID, proof of insurance, bill of sales if required and of course, money. The registration fees vary from state to state typically $5-$125. There's no federal road tax in the United States.

The Driving Test.

Every State has its own tests, although if you are American and you have passed in New York for example, you will not need to take a test again in Florida if you move. But you will have to pass a hearing and sight test. Although you will have to apply for a Florida license. The Division of Driver Licenses, Bureau of Field Operations, has driver license offices located throughout the state. Office hours are 8 a.m. to 5 p.m. Monday through Friday. Appointments are provided at all full service offices. Check Driver License Office Directory for addresses, telephone numbers, days and operating hours. Appointments are recommended.

You will be required to complete:

Hearing - Drivers applying for a license who are deaf, or cannot hear conversation spoken in a normal tone of voice, are restricted to driving with an outside rearview mirror which should be mounted on the left side of the vehicle, or wearing of a hearing aid.

Vision - Vision testing, using an eye machine located on the counters, and is conducted in all driver license offices. Visual acuity readings worse than 20/40 are referred to an eye specialist. Color blindness will not cause any special condition for licensing.

Road Signs - consists of 20 questions regarding road signs, with multiple choice answers.

Road Rules - consists of 20 questions regarding traffic laws and safety, with multiple choice answers.

Driving Test - You must provide a vehicle for the driving test. The vehicle must have a valid tag, proof of insurance, and pass a vehicle inspection. During the driving test, the examiner will observe your ability to control the vehicle and how well you obey traffic laws. These are pretty much the same for each state, however call in the local driving license office and get a handbook or see the website address at the back of the book.

Car Insurance.

Again each States requirements are different, but what they all have in common is that you need it and plenty of it. (Although some allow self- insurance or will let you take out a bond) If you hit another car, you have a 50% chance of them claiming an injury, they will soon be on the phone to the slip and fall lawyers. You can insure yourself for millions of dollars. It's good to have more cover than you need. In most cases you will not need it, but if you don't and you have an accident and its proven to be your fault, your spouse's fault or your child's fault you can be sued for not only the cost of replacement car, huge medical bills, lost of income, pain and suffering and anything else the lawyer can think up.

In Texas 2005 a small self employed man had a business repairing washing machines. As his business grew he employed a man and gave him a company van to use.

One weekend the employee got drunk and drove the van. You guessed it, he had an accident, and He caused a 25 year old doctor to suffer the loss of his hand. The claim of medical bills was just over $1,000,000 that's was not too bad, the business owners insurance could cover that. But then we come the loss of income: The doctor was a surgeon, it was estimated that he would have been able to earn $500,000 per year plus a yearly pay increase. He was also unable to drive that well, so a driver would be needed, extra help around the home, stress and pain. The total bill was sixty six million dollars. The small business owner lost his business, his home, his investments and his children had to drop out of college.

This is why if you are self employed you must form a limited company and have it set up correctly.

Liability Insurance includes bodily injury liability. In most States this is compulsory, although it may not include unlimited liability (Like the UK). Most States will set minimum levels for liability insurance, but these are often inadequate. I would recommend that you have at least $500,000 of cover as a minimum.

PIP. Personal Injury Protection or no fault insurance as it's also called. PIP pays the medical expenses of anyone injured when riding in your car, irrespective of fault. Depending on your provider and policy, it may also pay your medical bills when you or your family members are riding in someone else's vehicle, or even if you are hit by a car while walking. If you have comprehensive health insurance, you may not require this coverage. Discuss this with your insurance agent.

Uninsured Motorist Insurance. For protection for yourself against accidents with any uninsured motorist and hit and run's, you really should have uninsured motor insurance. The laws in various states regarding uninsured motor insurance are sometimes mandatory. Some states require insurance companies to include this in their basic policy cover against damage caused by motorist who are not insured. Uninsured motorist cover is usually equal to the minimum financial responsibility limits set by a state and is compulsory in some states. If you have collision insurance you may not need uninsured motor insurance.

Let's face it, Insurance is not going to be cheap, some states require other forms of insurance; Comprehensive Insurance for loss of your vehicle, some lease companies will require this or if your vehicle is on finance. (HP to the Brits reading this) Collision insurance to cover damage caused by you to your own vehicle, regardless of who was responsible for the damage. Collision insurance cover usually has a deductable excess. I would suggest you first hire a car for a month, while you have the rental car talk to at least two insurance companies and get quotes for all your family's needs. Some can be done on line. Overall insurance premiums in America are high, even higher for those under 27 and those who live in inner cities. Although many inner city dwellers no longer have a car. In New York there are now three generations of people who do not drive or own a car. Parking is very expensive; the traffic moves at a snail's space and as land is so expensive the houses and apartments do not all have garages. Many New Yorkers take the subway, a bus or a cab. If they drove to the movies or store they could not park, so what's the point?

If you have a driving record in America, you can expect to pay a premium of between $1250-$2250 per year for insurance and more for the extras mentioned above.

Buying a Car.

Detroit was the car capital of the World; unfortunately some say it's now the Arson capital of the world. Some parts are vey unsafe to walk during the day, let alone at night. But for years Detroit MI produced more vehicles per square mile than any place else on earth.

Recent years have seen demise in the sales of the traditional American cars such as Ford, Chevrolet, Buick, GM, Dodge, Jeep and Lincoln. Although all still producing cars, Toyota/Lexus, Nissan and Mazda now with factories in the United States dominate the market.

The majority of Americans lease a car. They feel it far better value to pay $200-$400 per month for 3 years and lease a car. At the end of the term, they turn the car in and lease another. Many CPA's (Certified Public Accountants) argue that it makes good business sense, while an equal number will argue against the idea, the choice is yours.

You will save approx $2000-$5000 if you buy a nearly new car rather than new, but again you must choose what's important for yourself. However what you can do is barter with the salesman. Don't worry, he/she will find you? I challenge you to try and walk across the forecourt of an Automobile center without being asked if you need help. Even if you reply, "I am just looking" they will then ask "anything in particular?" despite your objections, you will be lucky to get away with just a business card.

Be prepared to barter, the salesmen have one objective, sell a car NOW. They will offer all sorts for you to sign today. Use this as your defense and never ever pay the asking price. If you do not get at least 10% off, you have done a pretty poor job, and made a salesman very happy.

Once you have chosen your car and made a deal, you will then be passed onto a finance manager. Even if you are paying cash, they will ask for proof of insurance so they can get a tag for your car. The finance manager is also on commission and he has not had any yet, so it's his turn to make some money. He/she will offer you finance warranty and extended warranty. If you turn it down due to cost. Just like magic they find a lower rate of interest or better deal, if you sign up for a service program or warranty.

Used cars can also be purchased on eBay, autotrader.com, Craigslist.org and local papers. Plus many car sellers will stick a sign in the windows of a vehicle they are trying to sell.

The choice of vehicles is huge; you can buy nearly every make of vehicle (apart from French cars). The top selling vehicle in the United Sates in 2007 was the Ford F Series truck.

2008 Ford F150 FX4 *circa 2008*

The fall season is always a sweet spot for new car buying bargains. Because of sluggish auto sales, manufacturers offer a larger than usual consumer rebates and secret factory to dealer cash incentives to unload for example the 2008 cars, to make room for new 2009 models. Rebates change daily, so don't ask me why it's different when you look up new car rebates. If you've been waiting to buy a new car and get a great deal now is the time. Even Honda which normally does not offer incentives is getting in the game.

If the new car dealer does not have your car and options, they can order it from the factory. They DO NOT like doing this as the Salesman will want his sale today. The car should not cost more than the cars on the lot, but some dealers fool you. It does not cost dealers more, it's ordered as part of their weekly buying. Because new car factory orders don't sit on a lot waiting to sell, they cost dealers $0 on interest. New car dealers require a deposit of $500-$1000; try not to give more than $500. Don't pay deposits by check, use a credit card only. When the car comes in and they jack the price up $1000 telling you there was "a price increase", it's easy to dispute it off your credit card. But if you paid by check, they cashed it and you're stuck. There should be no fees; it's just a normal car deal. Lead time is 8 weeks to 6 months depending on the make and model. In the United States most people use Kelly's Blue Book for an idea on the price of a used or new car. Go to the website and put in make and model.

Used Cars

Dealers MUST attach a federal "Buyer's Guide" sticker on the window of each used car that tells you if the car is sold "As Is", or has a warranty and what obligations the dealer has. If the salesperson says the car has a warranty but the Buyers Guide sticker says "As Is", the sticker overrides the salesperson's lie. Unless there is time left on the 3 year manufacturer's warranty, you truly have no warranty if "As Is" is checked. Our number one complaint from consumers buying used cars from dealers, is the salesperson lied and told them the dealer will repair any failures, all the while the

"As Is" box was checked. The dealers then refused the repairs. The Buyers Guide tells you to have the car inspected by an independent mechanic before you buy, and to get all promises in writing. If the deal was conducted in Spanish, you are entitled to a Spanish language version of the Buyer's Guide. Look for weasel clauses in their warranty; don't just glance at the warranty form. If a used car dealer does not have Buyers Guide stickers on their cars, leave immediately!

Speed Limits

Speed limits vary in each state, most are signposted. Federal **Law does** have some recommended speed limits, such as 55 mph (88pmh) on freeways. This is increased to 65mph on interstate highways. But check local laws and signs. In Florida most interstates are 70mph, in CA the average is 55mph.

In different subdivisions they have their own speed limits and they have every number you can think of. I personally have seen areas that post 6 mph, 9 mph, 12mph, 20 mph, 22mph, 24, mph and 25mph. One can only assume that they have been dreamt up by the Homeowners association (HOA).

The lower speed limits should be observed at all times. If you are in a school district with flashing lights the speed limit is normally only 15 or 20mph. If you speed in this area expect to get a ticket and a large fine. On the interstates with 70mph posted most drivers do drive at 75-80mph with no problems. Go over this and you will be picked out via a helicopter, or State Trooper. If road workers are present, even state prisoners then the fines are doubled.

Getting pulled over by a law enforcement agency.

If you see flashing blue and red lights behind, pull over to the right. If you are on a busy road try and pull onto a side street or driveway. Open your window, turn off your engine and wait. Do not get out of the car until asked. Be polite and honest, if you are asked to show your license and documents, inform the officer that you will be reaching into your pocket or elsewhere in the car. In most cases you get a ticket you do not have to get out of the car.

Although rare some officers are shot by drug dealers and crooks at this point, so they will probably have a hand on top of their gun, this is normal. Even if the officer is wrong and said you did something you did not (Extremely rare) don't argue, there is absolutely no point, you may be able to get your day in court and protest (At your cost) but the judge will never take your side ever. You will end up with a bigger fine, court costs and a lot of stress and bother.

While driving and you see or hear any siren or flashing lights, pull over to the right, stop at the traffic lights even if green. If you are at red stop lights and an emergency vehicle comes up behind you, pull forward enough to allow it to pass, you will not get a ticket for going over the line. You may get a ticket for not moving. Just use common sense.

Hitchhikers.

Hitchhiking or even picking up hitchhikers in some states is illegal. I am not going to name the states. Just don't do it. America has over 300 million people most are very nice and safe. But as in all countries there is that 0.25% that are crazy, and will think nothing of stealing from you or a lot worse.

Drink Driving. DUI

Just as in your home country this is illegal and like most other countries it is a problem in the United States as well. You may have seen on the new many famous celebrities being found guilty of drunk driving and going to jail. Mel Gibson, Paris Hilton, and Kiefer Sutherland the star of 24 have all recently been charged and found guilty of DUI. (Driving under the Influence) Alcohol and drugs is estimated to be a factor in over 35% of all car wrecks. (Car accidents or crash) In 2007 1,674,655 people were arrested for DUI. Random sobriety tests (Breath test) are permitted in 46 states.

These tests can vary from reciting the alphabet, counting numbers backwards from 50, walking in a straight line, standing on one foot for a period of time and even touching the tip of your nose with an index finger with your eyes closed. They will also do breathe tests, blood tests and urine tests. You can refuse to give a blood or urine sample. However when you signed for your driving privilege on your license application, you also agreed that should you ever refuse such a test, you are volunteering your driving privilege and license to be revoked for any time from 6 months to a year.

If you are found to be DUI expect to be arrested, have a mug shot taken, that put in the local paper and local websites for all to see and get thrown in jail for a few hours, with all sorts of characters.

Car Wrecks (Accidents) what to do after an auto accident:

1)   Stay as calm as possible.

2)   Check for injuries. Life and health are more important than damage to vehicles. When in doubt, call an ambulance.

3)   If the accident is minor and there are no serious injuries, move cars to a safe place, rather than risk being in moving traffic.

4)   Turn on hazard lights. If warranted, and possible, use cones, warning triangles or flares for safety.

5)   Call the police, even if the accident is minor, failure to report an accident is a crime.

6)   Notify your insurance agent about the accident immediately.

7)   Don't sign any document unless it is for the police or your insurance agent

8)   Make immediate notes about the accident including the specific damages to all vehicles involved. If the name on the auto registration and/or insurance policy is different from the name of the driver, establish the relationship and jot it down. Get witness information, if possible, as well.

9)   Be polite, but don't tell the other drivers or the police that the accident was your fault, even if you think it was. Likewise, do not accuse the other drivers of being at fault at this time. Everyone is usually shaken up immediately after an accident, and it is wise to state only the facts. Limit your discussion of the accident to the insurance agent and the police. Even if the facts are embarrassing or detrimental to you, be truthful.

10)   If you have a camera handy, and it is safe to do so, it may be helpful to photograph the accident scene.

11)   If possible, do not leave the accident scene before the police officers and other drivers do.

12)   Finally, remember that while getting the facts is very important, investigating the accident should be left to the police officers and the insurance companies.

13)   When you caused the car crash, you have to file a claim with your insurance company.

14)   When the other driver caused the accident, you have the option to file a claim with your own insurance company or their company. When you file with your own it is called a "first-party" claim. If you file a claim with the other driver's company it is called a "third-party" claim. Insurance laws differ between the "first-party" and "third-party." It is vital you know what your rights and duties are in both cases. So read your policy. If you have questions, talk with your insurance company or the other driver's company.

OOP's *Circa 2008*

Gas Stations (Petrol)

At most US gas stations they sell 4 types of fuel. Unleaded, Mid-Grade and premium plus diesel. When gas hit $3.00 a gallon at the end of 2007 many Americans went crazy, they have been used to spending $1.80-$2.00. Many Americans are now re-thinking on what vehicles they buy. However gas is much cheaper than the cost of Europe.

To buy gas you can either pay at the pump with a credit or debit card or pay cash inside. If you want to pay via cash you have to pay first. My first experience back in the mid 1990's I went and asked for $10's worth of fuel. The attendant laughed at me, "Your never get ten bucks worth of fuel in that car buddy" So I paid $5 and filled it up. Today that will cost you $25.00 but when you consider the cost in Europe, it's still very cheap. Some gas stations have 2 price lists; one is for cash and the other for credit cards. You can bet the cash price will be in big bold letters, the credit card price is displayed on the pump itself. You will not know until you get out and look.

Some gas stations have Full-service sections the gas is approx $0.25 per gallon more, they will fill it up for you, check your oil level and expect a tip. You will probably get your windshield (Windscreen) cleaned as well, they are getting rare, but if you look for them you will find them, normally known as 'Mom & Pop' stores. (Family owned and run)

When driving in rural areas, you really should keep your tank full. Gas stations can get very sparse and if you come across one it may close on Sundays. If driving through a Saturday afternoon, you may have to book into a local motel for the weekend. In California it is an offense to run out of gas and you will be fined. Many Californian drivers carry a small gas can in the trunk.

Unlike Europe only 5% of small vehicles in the United States run on Diesel. They don't like it and let's face it; they have never had to worry about price and fuel consumption until now.

Section 27) Public Transport.

In major cities such as New York public transport is as good as London, Paris and Berlin. San Francisco CA also has a great public transportation system, mostly trams. However the rest of the United States does not, it's not needed as everyone drives. In Florida for example there is no public train system. You can't catch a train form Orlando to Miami.

There are two main kinds of bus service: The town and city bus services and the long distance bus services. They are sometimes called coaches.

Greyhound is the largest operator in the U.S. I am sure you have seen the silver Greyhound buses on an American made film. You are able to travel almost anywhere in the United States by Greyhound on an extensive network of scheduled routes and connections. They carry nearly 30 million passengers per year. No reservations are necessary when you travel with Greyhound. If you know the departure schedule, simply arrive at the terminal at least an hour before departure to purchase your ticket. Boarding generally begins 15 to 30 minutes before departure. Seating is on a first-come, first-served basis. Advance purchase tickets do not guarantee a seat. When Greyhound fills a regularly scheduled bus with passengers during times of peak demand, Greyhound plans for additional buses to accommodate passengers beyond the seating capacity of a single bus for any given schedule. However, our ability to add extra sections depends on the availability of buses, drivers and the number of passengers. When picking up passengers en route (such as at a rest stop), continuing passengers who de-boarded at the rest stop are given priority to re-board. Greyhound buses travel around the clock, so you can travel by day and enjoy the scenery through wide panoramic windows. Or, select a night service, and relax in a reclining seat with reduced interior lighting.

Most buses make intermediate stops to pick up additional passengers en route to their destinations. In addition to stops en route, buses make rest stops every few hours, and meal stops are scheduled as close to normal meal times as possible. If you prefer not to travel on a bus that includes multiple stops en route, be sure to ask your ticket agent about our express schedules, which are available on select routes. All Greyhound buses are equipped with air conditioning, an on-board restroom, reclining seats with headrests, footrests and tinted windows. Feel free to bring reading material, radio headsets and a small pillow for your comfort. Food and non-alcoholic beverages may be carried on board for personal consumption.

Radios, laptops and other electronic items may be carried on board, provided that they do not disturb fellow passengers and that headphones are used. (External power outlets are NOT available on Greyhound buses.) Greyhound buses are not equipped for movies on board, although some connecting carriers may offer this service.

Cabs (Taxis)

Taxi cabs are both loved and hated by New Yorkers. They serve as a quick and easy means of transportation across Manhattan, a route not amply served by the subways. The downside with having an abundance of cabs is the traffic that results. Most traffic-jams in mid-town are speckled with many of the over 10,000 yellow cabs that service the city. Hailing a Cab: The act of flagging down a cab is called "hailing"; there's not much to it, just stick out your arm. When the numbers on the roof of the cab are lit, then it is available. Yellow Medallion cabs are the only ones authorized to pick up hails. Avoid "gypsy" cabs at all costs. These are regular cars that will take you from place to place; they usually cost more than cabs and aren't as well regulated (or as safe). Officially, taxicabs can take on only four riders: 3 in the backseat, 1 in the front seat. Occasionally, the wider cabs will be willing to take 5 people, but they will usually ask the fifth person to duck down below the sight of the authorities. The famous large "Checker" cabs are pretty much a relic of the past, although you can still see some servicing the town at limousine service rates. Cab drivers should be able to speak English and to get a license they have to take a city test. Most have credit card machines in the cab.

New York drivers have a reputation of being the rudest and most aggressive drivers in the world. First of all, you have to know that 95% of new Yorkers are very abrupt and have no patience, it's a fast city and they expect things done now. A tourist lost driving around the city will get screamed at, honked, and shouted at by not only the cab drivers but anyone else trying to get from point A-B. If you ever need to make a complaint about a cab driver, make of a note of the cab number. It will be displayed on the dashboard, roof and receipt.

Section 28) Sports in America.

The good news is that they do not have any cricket. No longer will you have to endure hour upon hour of boredom. Sports play an important role in American society. They enjoy tremendous popularity but more important they are vehicles for transmitting such values as justice, fair play, and teamwork. Sports have contributed to racial and social integration and over history have been a "social glue" bonding the country together. Early Americans like Benjamin Franklin and President Thomas Jefferson stressed the need for exercise and fitness promoting for example running and swimming. In the 20th century, American presidents Theodore Roosevelt, Dwight D. Eisenhower and John F. Kennedy continued to encourage physical activity.

President Dwight D. Eisenhower founded the President's Council on Youth Fitness in 1956 to encourage America's youth to make fitness a priority. The Council later became the President's Council on Physical Fitness and Sports, including people of all ages and abilities and promoting fitness through sports and games. Today, the Council continues to play an important role in promoting fitness and healthy living in America.

The United States offers limitless opportunities to engage in sports - either as a participant or as a spectator. Team sports were a part of life in colonial North America. Native American peoples played a variety of ball games including some that may be viewed as earlier forms of lacrosse. The typical American sports of baseball, basketball and football, however, arose from games that were brought to America by the first settlers that arrived from Europe in the 17th century. These games were re-fashioned and elaborated in the course of the 19th century and are now the most popular sports in the United States. Various social rituals have grown up around athletic contests. The local high school football or basketball game represents the biggest event of the week for residents in many communities across the United States. Fans of major university and professional football teams often gather in parking lots outside stadiums to eat a "tailgate" picnic lunch before kickoff, and for parties in front of television sets in each other's homes during the professional championship game, the Super Bowl. Thousands of baseball fans flee the snow and ice of the North for a week or two each winter by making a pilgrimage to training camps in the South and Southwest to watch up close their favorite players prepare for the spring opening of the professional baseball season.

Many Americans watch sport rather than participate, although many belong to a fitness center or gym where state of the art equipment is common place. It is however true over 90% of Americans participate in sports at least once a month, either as participants or spectators. The major TV networks compete for TV rights to major league baseball, The National Football league and Ice Hockey State championships. The NFL can expect to collect more than $60 million form TV companies. TV does run the sports events and has a huge influence on what sport is popular in the United States. For example Soccer (Football to anyone outside America) is played by all schools and has many leagues and the USA team has a presence on the World arena. Most young children kick a ball around, however the game is played for 45 minutes each half without a break. The TV companies can't sell advertising in this slot and again the second half is another 45 minutes. Some Americans will say the game is slow, or they can't get into it, the truth is that the advertisers don't want it.

In the 2006 world cup, the TV Company went to a commercial break when the US team played and viewers across America missed their team score against Germany! After the break they returned and showed a repeat of the goal. While showing the repeat, Germany scored against the USA. It's hardly surprising the USA does not have a very big following for soccer.

Baseball

Baseball is a bat-and-ball sport played between two teams of nine players each. The goal of baseball is to score *runs* by hitting a thrown ball with a bat and touching a series of four markers called *bases* arranged at the corners of a ninety-foot square, or *diamond*. Players on one team (the *offense*) take turns hitting while the other team (the *defense*) tries to stop them from scoring runs by getting hitters *out* in any of several ways. A player on offense can stop at any of the bases and hope to score on a teammate's hit. The teams switch between offense and defense whenever the team on defense gets three outs. One turn on offense for each team constitutes an *inning*; nine innings make up a professional game. The team with the most runs at the end of the game wins. It is known as 'the beautiful game' and is really America's national sport.

There are two mayor baseball leagues with a total of 28 teams: The American League and the National League. Apart from Canada and a small league in Japan, it is only played in America. It's is a game of two teams of 9 players played on a 90ft square diamond, with four bases in the corners. The objective of each team is to win by scoring more runs than the opponent. Each fielder or catcher wears a glove. During the course of a game, alternate playing offense and defense. A "season" is played over the course of many months by a group of teams, called a league. Each team in the league plays all the other teams in the league a fixed number of times, though it is not always in round robin format. At the end of the season, the team with the most wins is the winner of the regular season.

The goal of a game is to score more points, which are called "runs" in the language of baseball, than the other team. Each team, usually composed of 9 or 10 players, attempts to score runs while on offense, by completing a tour of the bases, which form a square-shaped figure called a "diamond." A tour starts at home plate and proceeds counter-clockwise.

Baseball is played in a series of (usually 9) "innings", each of which is divided into two halves (called "top" and "bottom" in that order: hence the phrase bottom of the ninth). In each half-inning, the offensive team attempts to score runs until three of its players are put "out" (removed from play by actions of the defensive team; discussed below). After the third out, the teams switch roles for the other half of the inning. The "home" team plays defense first, and so plays defense in the top of every inning and offense in the bottom of every inning.

At the beginning of each half-inning, the nine defensive players arrange themselves on the field. One defensive player is called the "pitcher" and stands at the center of the diamond on a designated spot, called the mound or the rubber - a reference to the rectangular rubber plate at the center of the mound. Another defensive player is called the "catcher" and stands on the other side of home plate from the pitcher. Typically four more players are arranged along the lines between first, second, and third bases, and the other three are in the outfield.

Runs are scored as follows: starting at home plate, each offensive player attempts to earn the right to run (counterclockwise) to the next base (corner) of the diamond, then to touch the base at that corner, continuing on to each following base in order, and finally returning to home, whereupon a run (point) is scored. Often an offensive player will achieve a base but be forced to stop there; on future plays (usually in concert with other runners); the player may continue to advance, or else be put out.

A play begins with an offensive player called a "batter" standing at home plate, holding a bat. The batter then waits for the pitcher to throw a "pitch" (the ball) toward home plate, and attempts to hit the ball with the bat. If the batter hits the ball into play, the batter must then drop the bat and begin running toward 1st base. (There are other ways to earn the right to run the bases, such as "walks" or being hit by a pitched ball. See baseball for more.) The catcher catches pitches that the batter does not hit (either by choice or simple failure to make contact) and returns them to the pitcher.

If the batter fails to hit a well-pitched ball (one within the strike zone) or if he hits it so that it goes outside of the field of play it is called a "strike". (However, if the ball is hit over the outfield and exits the field there, it is instead (one type of) a "home run": the batter and all other offensive players on bases may complete a tour of the bases and score a run. This is the most desirable result for the batter.)

When a batter begins running, he or she is then referred to as a "runner". Runners attempt to reach a base, where they are "safe" and may remain there. The defensive players attempt to prevent this by putting the runners out using the ball; runners put out must leave the field (returning to the "bench" or "dugout", the location where all the other inactive players and managers observe the game).

American Football

American football, known in the United States simply as football, is a competitive team sport known for mixing complex strategy with intense physical play. The game is fast gaining popularity in Europe and in Japan. The object of the game is to score points by advancing the pointed-oval shaped ball into the opposing team's end zone. The ball can be advanced by carrying it (a running play) or by throwing it to a teammate (a passing play). You can score points in a variety of ways, including carrying the ball over the goal line, throwing the ball to another player past the goal line, tackling an opposing ball carrier in his own end zone, or kicking the ball through the goal posts on the opposing side. The winner is the team with the most points when the time expires and the last play ends.

If you want to watch the game, it's probably better to watch it on TV with an American who can explain the rules, after one game you will pick up the rules. The game is perfect for TV as it has lots of breaks.

The story of football began sometime during the 19th century in England when a soccer player, frustrated at using only his feet to manipulate the ball, decided to simply pick it up and run with it. Although it was clearly against the rules of soccer, other players soon found the new way of playing soccer appealing and thus, the sport of rugby was born. The new sport soon became a world-wide success that found its way into America by the mid-1800s. Played by many northeastern colleges, it was not long before Harvard University and Yale University met in Massachusetts in 1876 to formalize the rules to rugby that were similar to those in

England. There were differences however: instead of playing with a round ball, the schools opted for an egg-shaped and the game's name was changed from rugby to football. To finalize the meeting, an organization called the Intercollegiate Football Association (IFA) was created to preside over the Americanized sport.

Miami Dolphins player Dan Marino *Circa 1992*

Football was still mainly American rugby--much different from the popular sport known today. Over the course of three years starting in 1880, Yale player Walter Camp eventually convinced the IFA to change a series of rules in football to create a game that is very similar today. For that, Camp is considered by historians as the father of modern football.

The professional season runs from August to the end of December. In January we have the Super Bowl. This is played on a Sunday, the following Monday consistently has the highest number of calls in for sickness from employees. Usually results of too many beers and steak from the Bar-B Q. Over 40% of the country will watch the super bowl, it is a big tradition.

Ice Hockey

The sport was first played in Canada in the 1850's. In 1879 the first official Canadian league was formed. Often referred to simply as hockey in Canada and the United States, is a team sport played on ice. It is a speedy and physical sport. Ice hockey is most popular in areas that are sufficiently cold for natural, reliable seasonal ice cover, though with the advent of indoor artificial ice rinks it has become a year-round pastime at the amateur level in major metropolitan areas such as cities that host an NHL or other professional-league team. Florida of all places has a championship team Tampa Rays as they are called won the championship in 2003 and 2006 and has a huge following. It is one of the four major North American professional sports, and is represented by the National Hockey League (NHL) at the highest level, and the National Women's Hockey League (NWHL), the highest level of women's ice hockey in the world. It is the official national winter sport of Canada, where the game enjoys immense popularity, and is also the most popular spectator sport in Finland. Only six of the thirty NHL franchises are based in Canada, but Canadian players out number Americans in the league by a ratio of almost four to one. About thirty percent of the league's players are non-North American. The NHL competition runs from October to May. 78 Games are played in a season; tickets are always sold out at major games. At the end of the seasons the teams have playoffs for the Stanley Cup; this is played over a seven game series. It started in 1892;

the Stanley Cup was originally contested between Canada and America, but is now competed for by all 30 league teams. Violence in ice hockey has long been a controversial part of the sport. Most violent actions, such as kicking, hitting from behind, and illegal stick work, are penalized with suspensions or fines. Hockey, like other sports, has had incidents of violence which on some occasions have escalated to dangerous levels. Some examples are players deliberately injuring their opponents, brawls, fan involvement, and physical abuse of officials. Some fans admit that if there is not at least one brawl in a match, it's a disappointment. On the ice, referees may impose penalties for illegal activities. Off the ice, the NHL sometimes fines, suspends, or expels players. The criminal justice system has also been known to investigate, charge, and convict players.

Ottawa v Tampa Bay fight *Circa 2006*

In 2004 after repeated failed attempts at instigating a fight, Todd Bertuzzi of the Vancouver Canucks sucker-punched Steve Moore of the Colorado Avalanche from behind, knocking Moore unconscious. The pair then fell to the ice with Bertuzzi's weight crushing Moore face-first into ice and Bertuzzi continued to punch Moore, followed by several players from both teams further piling onto the mêlée. Moore sustained three fractured vertebrae, a grade three concussion, vertebral ligament damage, stretching of the brachial plexus nerves, and facial lacerations. Bertuzzi was charged by police, and given a conditional discharge after pleading guilty to assault causing bodily harm. His suspension resulted in a loss of $500,000 in pay and the Canucks were fined $250,000. Bertuzzi was re-instated in 2005, and Moore has made several (so far, last attempt December 2007) unsuccessful attempts at civil litigation.

Most major towns in The United States will have an ice rink and a hockey league, plus 20% of High schools also have access to a rink and will have teams.

Wrestling

This is a surprise to most immigrants to the United States. Over 40% of High schools have a wrestling team. It's nothing like the WWF that is shown on cable TV, but a serious sport.

State High school Championship California *circa 2007*

The object of the sport of wrestling is to put your opponent on his back and to pin your opponent. A pin (or fall) is when you put your opponent on his/her back with any part of both shoulders or both shoulder blades of your opponent in contact with the mat for two seconds. When you pin your opponent, the match is over and you are the winner. If nobody gets pinned, the winner is the wrestler who has scored the most points during the match.

Wrestling may be the ultimate contact sport, and it can be a startling sight, teenage boys grabbing girls' thighs, girls straddling boys, boys riding girls' backs and trying to flip them onto their backs. For the most part, girls who want to wrestle are slowly moving into the mainstream must practice with, and compete against, boys. Nationwide, about 18,000 high school girls wrestled last year, according to the National Federation of State High School Associations, nearly five times as many as a decade earlier. Those numbers are no doubt low, since many states failed to report girls' wrestling participation, but whatever the full count, it is dwarfed by the one million boys who wrestle. Now that women's wrestling is an Olympic sport, and, on some campuses, a college sport, girls' wrestling is poised to take off. There is a Catch-22: Without many girls, there can't be girls' teams, and without girls' teams, wrestling can't attract all that many girls. The legal status of coed wrestling is not entirely clear, but in a few scattered cases, courts have ruled that if there is no girls' team for them, they should be able to join boys' teams. This has caused a few problems, some boys have refused to wrestle with them and have forfeited the match. As you can imagine this causes a lot of upset among students and parents alike.

In Texas and Hawaii, and in some California schools, girls have their own teams. Girls' invitational tournaments, where girls compete individually, are becoming more common. Just this month, for the first time, the New York Mayor's Cup competition had a girls' division, albeit with only nine participants. On the other side, mothers of girl wrestlers say they worry about the cauliflower ears, broken noses and concussions. One thing that coaches, parents and wrestlers — both boys and girls — agree on is that sex is the last thing on wrestlers' minds as they pull and push and turn their partners, same sex or opposite. Girls' wrestling is not easy. The conditioning is grueling and intense, more so than for other sports. Since boys their age are usually stronger, only a few girls ever make varsity, let alone get to a state championship. And there is often parental resistance.

Basketball

The National Basketball Association (NBA) was formed in 1949 and has two leagues: the Western Conference with 14 teams divided between the Midwest and Pacific divisions, and the Eastern Conference with 15 teams divided between the Atlantic and Central divisions. The teams will play over 80 games during the season that runs from September to April. The teams at the top of the league play in a playoff. The playoffs are at the end of May and early June; these determine the NBA playoff teams and then the world championships.

Basketball is a huge sport many homes in cities and suburbs with have a hoop, either on a pole or attached to a wall of a home. This can be played solo or one on one. The official game is played on a court by two teams of five players. Points are made by shooting the ball through a high metal hoop and net at the opponent's end of the court. The large round ball used in this game is also called a basketball. It is a fast-paced competition played by men and women of all ages and ability. The basketball court on the playground or in a gymnasium is rectangular with regulation rims located

10 feet above the ground. In the early days, basketball was played with a soccer ball. Today's standard basketballs are orange to brown in color with an outer cover of leather or nylon and a pebbled (indented) surface for grip and control. In men's play, a regulation basketball is 29.5 to 30 in (74.9 to 76.2 cm) in circumference and 20 to 22 oz (567 to 624 g) in weight. Women's version can be slightly smaller and lighter in weight.

The game involves two five-player teams that play both offense and defense. With a few exceptions, basketball games whether they are played informally or in organized leagues follow generally consistent rules that have changed little since the game's invention in 1891. Games begin with a jump ball at center court; a referee throws the ball up while two opposing attempt to direct the ball to their teammates control. The basic offensive skills of basketball are passing, ball handling, shooting, and rebounding. Defensive skills include guarding opponents, blocking and positioning to defend the basket, using quickness to intercept or steal the ball, and rebounding missed shots.

The game has a huge following, although with the increasing cost in tickets sales due to the high wages paid to the players. This has given an increase in the following of college basketball, which many say is faster and more exiting.

Hunting & Guns

Too many this is not seen as a sport and seen as cruel and barbaric, but hunting that includes fishing is the largest participation sport in the United States. Even if you take away the he numbers of people who fish, Hunting with Guns and crossbow is still huge in the United States. They have their own television channel, where you can see hunters track a Bear, Deer, Buffalo, Fox, Coyote, Moose, Alligator, Duck, Wolf, Hogs, Wild Turkey and shoot it. After they pose with the dead animal for pictures. Some animals are protected such as the Florida Panther and some bears in certain parts of the country.

Hunting is now a science; the items hunters can use are state of the art, Satellite tracking and Infrared just to name a few. Guns can shoot over a mile with laser sights, it's hard to miss. Whether you are for or against it, hunting is a multi-billion dollar sport and it will not go away. It's part of American tradition and way of life. If you eat meat and try a fresh Buffalo steak or spit roasted wild hog you will know what I mean, the flavor and texture is something you will never discover from animals produced on a farm.

The fishing scene is America is the largest in the world. You can fish for anything, Salmon, Trout, Bass, Tuna or Shark the list goes on and on. Depending on what state you are in, fishing of some form is available.

The right to own a firearm is embedded in the American psyche like a splinter of flint, jagged and immovable. It all goes back to the Founding Fathers who in 1791 amended the new American constitution with the following words: "A well regulated militia, being necessary to the security of a free state, the right of the people to keep and bear arms, shall not be infringed." This amendment was drawn up by people living in a precarious agrarian society unrecognizable to modern Americans, when communities needed guns to hunt and to protect themselves from Indians and outlaws.

The gun lobby has plucked out the phrase "the right of the people to keep and bear arms" and used it ever since to beat down every serious attempt at gun control in America by claiming a violation of the constitution. Members of the great American gun culture who actively enjoyed their sport and celebrated their firearms heritage were once considered the backbone of America, both for their militarily valuable shooting skills and for their patriotism. Decades of deliberate attacks by politicians and the media have slowly relegated this important group to the status of a subculture that now feels out of place and at war with its own government.

The right to own a firearm is embedded in the American psyche like a splinter of flint, jagged and immovable. Colt 45 *Circa 1983*

Prior to 1934 there were no federal gun control laws. There was only an odd assortment of gun laws in various states and cities which were intended to disarm racial minorities and immigrants. As far as the federal government was concerned, anyone was free to buy a machine gun or even a cannon, and the level of gun crime was relatively low. Since the National Firearms Act was signed into law in 1934, the number of gun control laws at all levels of government have multiplied exponentially. So has the overall crime rate, which some argue is a direct result of gun control laws that discourage self-defense.

Although none of these laws reduced crime, each new law creates another way that a well intentioned gun owner can inadvertently end up in prison or ruined by legal costs. Some have been killed in raids by government agents. Much like laws passed to promote the failed war on drugs, each new gun law gives the police additional powers that threaten basic constitutional rights.

America's lawful gun owners are painfully aware of these facts. Since gun laws don't reduce crime, they wonder, what is the real purpose? This question has led to numerous theories that attempt to explain why the "ruling elite", which includes the media and many politicians, would want to eliminate civilian gun ownership in America. Gun control is one of the most fraught issues in the USA. It may be incomprehensible to those outside the United States, but guns, like abortion, occupy a unique, high-profile position in US politics. The right to own a gun and defend oneself is central to the American identity and stems in part from the nation's frontier history. Guns were integral to America's westward expansion, enabling settlers to guard themselves from Indians, animals and foreign armies. Citizens assumed much responsibility for self-protection. The 'Wild West' mentality is still evident in the US psyche today. A notable example was President Bush's famous rhetoric after the September 11 terrorist attacks that he wanted Osama bin Laden 'dead or alive'. The importance of guns also derives from the role of hunting in American culture. In the nation's early years, hunting was essential for food and shelter, and today remains very popular as both a sport and a way of life in many parts of the country.

Other Sports.

Just about every other sport is played in the United States. America has more Golf courses than any other country, and 32 x more swimming pools than any other country in the World. Athletics, Archery, Badminton, Billiards, BMX, Body building, Bowling, Boxing, Canoeing & Kayaking, Chess, Cycling, Darts, Diving, Fencing, Frisbee League, Gymnastics, Handball, Horse riding, Ice Skating, Jai Alai, Lacrosse, Lawn bowls, Martial Arts, Polo, Pool, Racing, Rollerblading, Sailing, Skateboarding, Softball, Surfing, Table Tennis, Tennis, Volleyball, Weightlifting and Windsurfing to name a few.

Section 29) Buying or Renting a Home in America.

Whether you see owning a home as an investment or as a liability, it will cost thousands of dollars and therefore you should get it right. Again please remember that all 50 states have different laws, this includes real estate and transactions. You do not however need 50 books, as the laws don't differ that much. A Real estate agent or Realtor as they are known are a necessary fact of life when you are buying a home. You can try and buy a home direct from a seller, you will see it advertised as 'For sale by Owner' but these often go wrong and can cost a small fortune to put the matter right. All real estate licensees are not the same. Only real estate licensees who are members of the NATIONAL ASSOCIATION OF REALTORS are properly called realtors. They proudly display the REALTOR logo on the business card or other marketing and sales literature. Realtors are committed to treat all parties to a transaction honestly. Realtors subscribe to a strict code of ethics and are expected to maintain a higher level of knowledge of the process of buying and selling real estate. An independent survey reports that 84% of home buyers would use the same realtor again.

Your realtor can help you determine your buying power that is, your financial reserves plus your borrowing capacity. If you give a realtor some basic information about your available savings, income and current debt, he or she can refer you to lenders best qualified to help you. Most lenders, banks and mortgage companies offer limited choices. Plus a realtor has many resources to assist you in your home search. Sometimes the property you are seeking is available but not actively advertised in the market, and it will take some investigation by your agent to find all available properties. A realtor can assist you in the selection process by providing objective information about each property. Agents who are realtors have access to a variety of informational resources. Realtors can provide local community information on utilities, zoning. Schools, etc. There are two things you'll want to know. First, will the property provide the environment I want for a home or investment? Second, will the property have resale value when I am ready to sell?

Your realtor can help you negotiate. There are myriad negotiating factors, including but not limited to price, financing, terms, date of possession and often the inclusion or exclusion of repairs and furnishings or equipment. The purchase agreement should provide a period of time for you to complete appropriate inspections and investigations of the property before you are bound to complete the purchase. Your agent can advise you as to which investigations and inspections are recommended or required. Also a realtor provides due diligence during the evaluation of the property. Depending on the area and property, this could include inspections for termites, dry rot, asbestos, faulty structure, roof condition, septic tank and well tests, just to name a few. Your realtor can assist you in finding qualified responsible professionals to do most of these investigations and provide you with written reports. You will also want to see a preliminary report on the title of the property. Title indicates ownership of property and can be mired in confusing status of past owners or rights of access. The title to most properties will have some limitations; for example, easements (access rights) for utilities. Your realtor, title company or attorney can help you resolve issues that might cause problems at a later date. A realtor can guide you through the closing process and make sure everything flows together smoothly. And finally a realtor can help you in understanding different financing options and in identifying qualified lenders.

How to find a Realtor:

Most will find you, I personally know 12 realtors, I live in a street of 19 homes and 4 owners are also realtors. Many realtors work part time. Teachers, Police officers etc also work as realtors in spare time. One of the first things to look for when selecting a realtor is their affiliation with a trade group such as the NATIONAL ASSOCIATION OF REALTORS. This affiliation is no guarantee but it does offer some measure of assurance that the realtor follows certain professional codes of standard. Every Realtor will have access to the MLS (Multiple Listing System). The MLS is a group of private databases which allows real estate brokers representing sellers under a listing contract to widely share information about properties with real estate brokers who may represent potential buyers or wish to cooperate with a seller's broker in finding a buyer for the property. There is no single authoritative "MLS", and no universal data format. The many local and private databases some of which are controlled by single associations of realtors or groupings of associations (which represent all brokers within a given community or geographical area) or by real estate brokers are collectively referred to as the MLS because of their reciprocal access agreements.

Seen most widely in the US and Canada but spreading to other countries in a variety of forms, the MLS combines the listings of all available properties that are represented by brokers who are both members of that MLS system and of NAR or CREA, (the National Association of Realtors in the US or the Canadian Real Estate Association).

The purpose of the MLS is to enable the efficient distribution of information so that, when a real estate agent is introduced to a potential home buyer, s/he may search the MLS system and retrieve information about all homes for sale in a given area or price range, whether under a listing contract by that agent's brokerage or by all participating brokers.

In North America, the MLS systems are governed by private entities, and the rules are set by those entities with no state or federal oversight, beyond any individual state rules regarding real estate. MLS systems set their own rules for membership, access, and sharing of information, but are subject to nationwide rules laid down by NAR or CREA. An MLS may be owned and operated by a real estate company, a county or regional real estate Board of Realtors or Association of Realtors, or by a trade association. Membership of the MLS is generally considered to be essential to the practice of real estate brokerage.

Most MLS systems restrict membership and access to real estate brokers (and their agents) who are appropriately licensed by the state (or province); are members of a local Board or Association of Realtors; and are members of the trade association (e.g., NAR or CREA).

A person selling his/her own property - acting as a For Sale by Owner (or FSBO) - cannot put a listing for the home directly into the MLS. Similarly, a properly licensed broker who chooses to neither join the trade association nor operate a business within the associations' rules cannot join the MLS. However it is possible to do a Google search and find a local agent on the web and use the system. This way you are able to do searches yourself.

When choosing a realtor make sure you get at least 2 recommendations of if you are new in town, interview at least two realtors. I would not work with anyone whose credentials I have not checked out. It's very easy to get a realtors license, so you want to ensure you are getting the best.

The seller pays the commission, typically 6%. When they list that house they are guaranteed 3% as the selling agent. If they also find the buyer, they also collect the other 3%. If you have a realtor he or she will get the 3%. On a 2 million dollar home, that's a lot of money, but unlike Europe, they do really work for it. One point to remember is the more you pay for the home the larger the cut of commission they get. Do not ask for advice on how much to offer! That's just like waving a blank check in front of them. Offer at least 20% off the asking price. There is a way to avoid the conflict of interest and that is to use a buyer's agent who works exclusively for you and will charge you a reduced or flat fee. While interviewing the realtor, you need to ask: How many homes have you sold in the last 12 months? How many have you helped purchase? They all have to start somewhere, but you need to ask how long they have been a realtor and if it's a full time job. Some very good realtors arrive in a BMW or Mercedes wearing a Rolex etc, they are very successful, as it's the seller who pays them and not you as the buyer, I would recommend you use someone like this. They are obviously good at their job. Once you are happy with your choice of realtor, you are now ready to start looking for properties.

Viewing Homes.

In the United States viewing is always done with your realtor. If you are flying over to the States and have a limited stay arrange the viewings in advance, you can typically see 5 -7 homes in a day, more if they are on one subdivision. You will also see 'Open Houses' this is where the seller opens up the home for a given period of any given day. They should have staged the home, it should be clean and smelling fresh, the seller's realtor will normally prepare this.

If you are looking as a lot of homes like this, take a notepad and file, You will be given details on each property by your realtor, so file them so you can identify each house, you can also take extra pictures or use a video, and then without the pressure of your realtor, home owners and possibly the sellers realtors, you can make up your mind and discuss with your partner. You might also find yourself identifying desirable amenities that you hadn't thought of. Make a note of them. With all your information in front of you, you can begin the process of elimination and most importantly choosing the right house for you.

Do not at any point during the inspection sound too positive; do not discuss it until you are alone. This is the number one rule, I have seen some couples look at a house and heard the lady informing her husband, "Oh, This is just perfect" can we get it?" If your realtor, the seller's realtor or worse of all the sellers hear this, how do you think they will act when you try to negotiate the price?

How to be successful in putting in an offer.

If you have followed the advice so far and you did not give anything away while looking, now you are ready to put in an offer. In America an offer is binding, however you can make an offer subject to certain terms, I will cover later. Remember your realtor is not a friend this is business and treat the whole purchase like a business. Inform your realtor you like three homes, but you will try an offer on one home.

This is the home you really want, put an offer in at least 20% less than the asking price. You will also have to give a check for deposit, normally $1000. Show them that you are serious and give a deposit check of at least $7500. Your realtor will ask you, "what would you like to get if for?" Reply the price I have just offered. Do not give anything away. Also make the offer open for only 24 hours, ignore the realtor if they want longer, and remind the realtor you have other properties in mind. **DO NOT** be concerned about hurting the nice seller's feelings, chances are, even if you buy the property you will never see them again.

The offer is a binding contract, once accepted you have to go through with the purchase, or you will lose your deposit and risk getting sued. However you can include in your offer the following: Subject to inspections, Subject to agreement with partner: this is a great get out clause. If your partner does not agree, you can withdraw. But who is your partner Tom? It could be your dog or your cat or your spouse. It's not illegal, if your dog Tommy is your partner and he does not want to buy the home, you have a get out. You will not have to say who your partner is. I would not inform them, you may get put in a padded cell.

Expect your first offer to be rejected. Example: House for sale $350,000 you offered (less 20%) $280,000 they will probably come back with a counter offer. Example $330,000 Plus they will now put pressure on you and only give you 24 hours to respond. Your realtor will contact you and give the news and ask what your counter offer is? Inform him or her you will think about it. After this do nothing, ignore calls from your realtor and get on with your business. The counter offer will expire, let the weekend come and go, the sellers will discuss how maybe they should have put in a lower offer. On the Tuesday contact your realtor, inform him or her to put in another offer this time go just a little higher, maybe $295,000. Inform your realtor they have 24 hours, if not you want to put an offer in on another property. Your realtor will submit the offer and inform the seller's realtor that if it is rejected, you will be putting in an offer on another property. The seller's realtor (at risk of no commission) will put pressure on the sellers, informing them the market is slow and maybe they should consider the offer. This works 9 times out of 10, remember you can always go higher, but not lower. Once your offer is accepted you move onto the next step.

Home buyers report.

In most cases, purchasing real estate is the largest investment that you will ever make. Gaining insight into the general condition of the building, major deficiencies in any of the components, the age of its systems and corresponding life expectancies, the need for repairs and the positive attributes of the property (i.e.: new roof, low maintenance exteriors and upgrades) gives you the necessary facts to make an informed buying decision. The simple axiom is that the more you know about the property - the less your exposure to the risks inherent in purchasing the property. Starting at the exterior of the property, the inspector will visually inspect the roof, flashing, chimneys, gutters, and downspouts. The inspector will then inspect the siding, trim, windows, doors, decks, walkways and driveways. Drainage issues, retaining walls and patios will be inspected as to any negative impact that they may pose on the building.

After the inspector has completed his survey of the exterior he will inspect the visible framing members in the attic and basement for signs of structural defects and prior repairs.

The inspector will also visually inspect the electrical system, the heating and cooling systems, the plumbing, insulation, and appliances. While these areas are being observed the inspector will note any deficiencies in the interior components of the home. In addition to noting any visible defects, throughout the inspection, the inspector will explain how the various systems of the home operate and give you information on how to maintain the home. It is a good idea to bring a pad of paper and any questions that you may have to the inspection so the inspector can address your concerns during the on-site walk-through.

After the inspection is complete, the inspector will produce a written report that describes the systems and components of the home and reports the defects and repairs that were noted during the inspection.

The on-site inspection averages to 2 to 3 hours, but can vary based on the size, age and general condition of the home being inspected. Smaller properties will take less time, while large and complex properties will take longer.

Do I need an inspection if I am building or purchasing a new home?

Absolutely. Contrary to what many people think, brand new homes and homes under construction should be inspected regardless of whether they will be conveyed with a builder's warranty. Further, the inspections that are completed by local code enforcement officials are focused primarily on a narrow set of code compliance issues and are not nearly as broad or inclusive.

Our inspectors routinely observe structural, heating, cooling, roofing, exterior, plumbing and interior defects in new homes that may go unnoticed by both the builder and purchaser until they become a substantial problem. *Part 1 -* The inspector will visit the property when the foundation has been poured, but prior to backfill and inspect the foundation, footings, basement slab preparation work and foundation drainage system. The inspector's findings will be detailed in writing and provided in duplicate to the client so a copy can be forwarded to the builder. *Part 2 -* The building will be inspected prior to the installation of the insulation. The inspector will inspect the framing, sheathing, roofing materials and the rough electrical, heating and plumbing work. Again, the inspector's findings will be detailed in writing and provided in duplicate to the client so a copy can be forwarded to the builder. *Part 3 -* When the building is completed, the inspector will inspect the exterior, roof, gutters, chimneys, flashings, siding, trim, doors and site. He will also inspect the finished heating, cooling, electrical, plumbing, and interior systems.

Should I attend the inspection?

If at all possible, yes. Valuable information regarding the condition of the home and its systems can be gained from spending just a few hours with one of our inspectors. Information on the proper operation and maintenance of the building and its systems is also given at the time of the physical inspection. If you cannot attend the inspection, your inspector will complete the inspection, produce the written report and call you to discuss the home and the items contained in the report.

Loan types: Loans can be classified in various ways based on their length, their requirements for security, and their repayment schedules.

Adjustable Rate Loan - An adjustable rate loan has provisions to change the interest rate at pre-specified points in time based on changes in a market index, a lender's cost of funds or other factors as determined by the lender.

Balloon loan - Loans with periodic payments during the term of the loan, with the remaining balance due at maturity. Payments may be interest only or interest plus some portion of the principal. The balloon payment is the final payment of a balloon loan and contains the unpaid balance, which may amount to most of the original loan amount.

Blended rate loan - A refinanced loan where the lender blends the interest rate of the existing loan with the lenders current interest rate for new loans.

Bridge loan - A temporary, single-payment loan used by creditors to abridge the time period between the retirement of one loan and the issuance of another. An example is a loan used for the down payment on a new real estate purchase.

Construction loan - A loan where money is advanced as construction takes place and money is needed.

Demand loan - A loan with no specific maturity date. The lender may demand payment on the loan at any time.

Fixed rate loan - A loan that bears the same interest rate until loan maturity.

Intermediate term loan - A loan to be repaid (or amortized) over a period of 18 months to 10 years, with 3 to 5 years being most common. Intermediate-term loans typically are used to finance machinery, equipment, automobiles, trucks, breeding livestock, improvements, and other durable, yet depreciable, assets.

Long-term loan - A loan to be repaid (or amortized) over a period of time exceeding 10 years, with 20- to 30-year loans being common when financing real estate.

Non-recourse loan - A loan obligation that can be collected by the secured party only by taking the property used as collateral. In other words, the borrower has no obligation to repay other than what was used as collateral and the secured party cannot collect more than the collateral even if the remaining loan amount is more than the value of the collateral.

Overline loan - A loan in excess of a financial institution's legal lending limit to any one borrower in which the institution has enlisted the services of another lender to participate in the loan.

Operating loan - A short-term loan (i.e., less than one year) to finance crop production, livestock production, inventories, accounts receivable and other operating or short-term liquidity needs of a business.

Participation loan - A loan that requires interest plus a portion of the profits as payment.

Purchase money loan - A loan used to purchase property that serves as its own collateral.

Recourse loan - A loan obligation where the borrower is liable for the full amount of the remaining balance of the loan, even if the collateral value is less than the remaining balance.

Rollover loans - Short-term loans obtained with the anticipation that the loan will be renewed at its due date, rather than repaid.

Secured loan - A loan on which some asset is pledged as collateral to ensure payment of the loan.

Self-liquidating loans - A loan which will be repaid from the sale of the assets originally purchased with the loan funds.

Short term loan - A loan scheduled to be repaid in less than a year.

Signature loan - A loan for which no collateral is pledged.

Single payment loan - A loan in which the entire amount owed is due in one payment at maturity.

Take-out-loan - A permanent loan arrangement to replace a construction loan. Normally a long-term loan is implemented when the construction of a facility is completed. The facility may serve as collateral for the new loan.

Term loan - A loan that requires only interest payments until the last day of its life, at which time the full amount borrowed is due.

Tiered loans - Loans grouped according to the risk characteristics of borrowers. Higher risk classes generally are charged higher interest rates to compensate the lender for carrying the credit risk.

Unsecured loan - A loan for which there is no collateral required. The loan is backed up only by the promise of the borrower to repay.

Mortgages:

Blanket mortgage - A lien on more than one parcel of real estate.

First mortgage - A real estate mortgage that has priority over all other mortgages on a specified piece of real estate.

Graduated payment mortgage - A type of delayed payment mortgage where the payments increase over time.

Second mortgage - The use of two lenders in a real estate mortgage in which one lender holds a first mortgage on the real estate and another lender holds a second mortgage. The first mortgage holder has first claim on the borrower's mortgaged property and assets in the event of loan default and foreclosure or bankruptcy.

Shared appreciation mortgage - A financing arrangement for real estate in which the lender reduces the interest rate on the loan in return for a stipulated share of the appreciated value of the land being financed at a designated time in the future. The risk of land value appreciation is shared between lender and borrower, and the lender's compensation from value appreciation generally occurs through refinancing in which the loan balance is increased by the amount of the shared appreciation.

Finance and Credit and Social security numbers.

Circa 1983

If you are paying cash, great this will help with your barging. However you may require finance.

If you are buying a home in the United States as a second home, it can be an advantage to mortgage your home in your home country. For a start it will be very cheap to set up, if you stay with the same lender there will be no legal fees or land registry fee for the additional loan. There may not even be an arrangement fee. If you go to a new lender, they may offer you special deals and lower rates. Plus the loan payments will be in your countries currency and coming direct from your income. This will not be affected by fluctuations in currency exchange. Plus you should be familiar with your own countries mortgages. Before I cover US mortgages you need to look at Social security numbers. (SSN)

What Is a Social Security Card or Number?

A Social Security card contains a unique number, a Social Security Number, issued to you by the Social Security Administration (SSA). The Social Security Number (SSN) is used by government agencies, schools, and businesses to identify people in their computer systems. It is a very important identifying number and will stay with you for the rest of your life. Every working person and taxpayer in the United States must have a social security number.

The nine-digit Social Security number is divided into three parts. The first three numbers generally indicate the state of residence at the time a person applies for his or her first card. The middle two digits of a Social Security number have no special significance, but merely serve to break the numbers into blocks of convenient size. The last four characters represent a straight numerical progression of assigned numbers.

Types of Social Security Cards Issued

When you receive a Social Security card, it will be one of three types:

The first type of card is the card most people have, and has been issued since 1935. It shows the person's name and Social Security number, and it lets the person work without restriction. SSA issues it to U.S. citizens and permanent resident aliens.

The second type of card bears the legend "NOT VALID FOR EMPLOYMENT." SSA issues it to people from other countries who are lawfully admitted to the United States without U.S. Citizenship and Immigration Services (USCIS) work authorization, but who need a number because of a federal, state or local law requiring a Social Security number to get a benefit or service.

SSA began issuing the third type of card in 1992. It bears the legend "VALID FOR WORK ONLY WITH INS AUTHORIZATION." It is issued to people who are admitted to the United States on a temporary basis with USCIS (formerly INS) authorization to work

If you need a Social Security number, want to replace your lost or stolen card, or want a card showing your new name, you will need to file Form SS-5 (Application for a Social Security Card) with your nearest Social Security office. This service is free. Forms are available online, or at your nearest Social Security office, or by calling Social Security's national toll free number: 1-800-772-1213.

Read the instructions on the form carefully. You will need to provide original supporting documents, including proof of your lawful alien status, along with the form. If you are age

18 or older and have never been assigned a number before, you must apply in person. Otherwise, you have a choice to send your application and supporting documents by mail. In this case, the Social Security office will return your documents to you. If you do not want to mail your original documents, take them to the nearest Social Security office.

If you do not have permission to work in the U.S., you will need to provide a letter, on letterhead stationery (no form letters or photocopies), from the government agency requiring you to get a number. The letter must specifically identify you as the applicant, cite the law requiring you to have a Social Security number, and indicate that you meet all the agency's requirements except having the number.

If you are assigned a number for non-work purposes, you cannot use it to work. If you use it to work, the Social Security Administration may inform the U.S. Citizenship and Immigration Services.

There is no law either authorizing or prohibiting the use of Social Security numbers by organizations other than government agencies. In increasing numbers, government agencies, schools, and businesses rely on Social Security numbers to identify people in their computer systems. Your Social Security number is usually needed when opening a bank account, registering for school, on tax documents, and for payroll purposes. Banks and other financial institutions use the numbers to report interest earned on accounts to the Internal Revenue Service (IRS), and government agencies use Social Security numbers in computer operations to stop fraud and abuse.

Providing your Social Security number to organizations other than the SSA does NOT give them access to your Social Security records. The privacy of your records is guaranteed unless 1) disclosure to another government agency is required by law or 2) the information is needed to conduct Social Security or other government health or welfare programs.

Nevertheless, you generally should not use your Social Security number as an identification card. Keep it in a safe place and do not let anyone else handle it.

Retirement Benefits

Social Security pays monthly retirement benefits to more than 30 million retired workers and their families. More than 9 out of 10 Americans who are age 65 or older get Social Security benefits.

Full retirement benefits are now payable at age 65, with reduced benefits available as early as age 62. The age for full benefits will gradually rise in the future, until it reaches age 67 in 2027 for people born in 1960 or later. (Reduced benefits will still be available at age 62.)

Financial advisers often tell people that, when they retire, they will need about 70 percent of pre-retirement income to live comfortably. By itself, Social Security replaces about 60% of the pre-retirement earnings of a low wage earner, 42% of an average wage earner, and 26% of a high wage earner. However as in your home country by 2018, no government in the western world will be able to afford to pay retirement benefits to everyone who has paid in. It will be means tested, so either save hard or do nothing.

Credit Scores,

Even if you are Richard Branson when you move to the United States your record score will be nil. The best you can get is 800. It's easy to obtain a credit score; it will just take 6-12 months. Go to a bank open an account and ask for a pre-approved credit card. This will cost you approx $250 and your card will have a limit of approx $200. Use it 2-3 times a month but never use more than 50% of your limit. Complete an automated payment form, so the card is cleared every month. After six months your limit will be increased to $1000-$1500, keep doing the same and after 12 months you will have a score of approx 675-700.

Your credit score is a number generated by a mathematical algorithm, a formula based on information in your credit report, compared to information on tens of millions of other people. The resulting number is a highly accurate prediction of how likely you are to pay your bills. If it sounds arcane and unimportant, you couldn't be more wrong. Credit scores are used extensively, and if you've gotten a mortgage, a car loan, a credit card or auto insurance, the rate you received was directly related to your credit score. The higher the number, the better you look to lenders. People with the highest scores get the lowest interest rates.

Scoring categories

Lenders can use one of many different credit-scoring models to determine if you are creditworthy. Different models can produce different scores. However, lenders use some scoring models more than others. The FICO score is one such popular scoring method.

Its scale runs from 300 to 850. The vast majority of people will have scores between 600 and 800. A score of 720 or higher will get you the most favorable interest rates on a mortgage, according to data from Fair Isaac Corp., a California-based company that developed the first credit score as well as the FICO score. Currently, each of the three major credit bureaus uses their own version of the FICO scoring method -- Equifax has the BEACON score, Experian has the Experian/Fair Isaac Risk Model and TransUnion has the EMPIRICA score. The three versions can come up with varying scores because they use different algorithms. (Variance can also occur because of differences in data contained in different credit reports.)

That could change, depending on whether a new credit-scoring model catches on. It's called the Vantage Score. Equifax, Experian and TransUnion collaborated on its development and will all use the same algorithm to compute the score. Consumers can order their Vantage Scores online at Experian's Web site for $6. Its scoring range runs from 501 to 990 with a corresponding letter grade from A to F. So, a score of 501 to 600 would receive an F, while a score of 901 to 990 would receive an A. Just like in school, A is the best grade you can get.

What's the big deal?

No matter which scoring model lenders use, it pays to have a great credit score. Your credit score affects whether you get credit or not, and how high your interest rate will be. A better score can lower your interest rate.

The difference in the interest rates offered to a person with a score of 520 and a person with a 720 score is 4.36 percentage points, according to Fair Isaac's Web site. On a $100,000, 30-year mortgage, that difference would cost more than $110,325 extra in interest charges, according to Bankrate.com's mortgage calculator. The difference in the monthly payment alone would be about $307

Circa 2003

Typical Florida home, Standard, 3 bed, 2 bath, **double garage, 19 ft ceilings and pool. Most pools have a mesh frame as shown, to keep out leaves and bugs.** *Circa 2003*

United States Mortgages

If you are living in the United States or your home country, if you have a deposit, I can get you a mortgage. I have worked as a Mortgage broker in the UK for over 10 years and 6 years in the United States. However, I am not here to sell you a mortgage, just to give advice.

If you can find 25% deposit of the purchase price or valuation (appraisal) whichever is the lower, you can get a mortgage. Worldsavings, Chase finance, and Wachovia are just a few that come to mind. The rates are competitive and they are quick to arrange. In the business we call them Non-Resident mortgages, but they can be used for residents just the same. If you default the mortgage company will keep the house and the 25% equity. If you are working how much you can afford in payments, your monthly payment should never exceed more than 28% of your gross income.

The concept of mortgages in the United States is the same as the rest of the world. It is secured against the land or buildings. If you do not keep the payments the bank will foreclose on you, (Repossess).

In the United States it's common to take out a mortgage for 30 years, unlike the UK where it is normally 25 years. However one big difference I found strange. In the United States you are not allowed to use borrowers age to determine if the loan can be agreed or not. In the UK you can't take out a mortgage that will pass age 68 unless you can prove that you have retirement plans/ pensions that will provide enough income to keep up the repayments. In the United States an 85 year old man can take out a 30 year mortgage if he/she meets the normal criteria.

The amounts you can borrow will depend on the lender, Unlike Europe what is typically based on 3 times income plus 1 year's income of a spouse. In the US every different lending institution is different. Therefore DO NOT go to a bank for a mortgage. They may turn you down or sell a product that may not be right for you. A bank can only offer its products, and can't offer products from the bank next door or even a bank in another state. Always use an independent mortgage broker (I had to get that plug in).

Mortgage Broker

A licensed Independent Mortgage Broker can offer you rates and Plans from every financial institution in that State and lenders in other states that lend in your state. More than half of all the real estate loans made in the United States originate from mortgage brokers. A mortgage broker is a middle-person who brings together lenders and borrowers. Mortgage brokers each work with different lenders, sometimes 200 or more. It's important to ask about the variety of products offered as this will vary from broker to broker. Fees are paid by the buyer or lender or both.

Loans at "par" mean the buyer is not paying a fee. Yield-spread premiums (YSPs) are typically disclosed at closing and paid by the lender. Mortgage brokers can also operate as "up-front" mortgage brokers, meaning they will negotiate a fee directly with the buyer in exchange for shopping for the lowest (wholesale) interest rate & fees.

Mortgage Bankers

Mortgage bankers, as you may have guessed, work for a bank. They may represent more than one bank but the loans they make are bank loans, funded by the bank. Fees are generally not negotiable and are set by bank policy. Loan products are limited to those the bank offers.

Be aware that the Mortgage banker may not be licensed. It's not a required in every state.

Commercial Banks

Citigroup, Bank of America, and Wells Fargo are good examples of well known commercial banks. Commercial banks offer a wide variety of services. In fact, you probably have a bank like this in your neighborhood. Primary source

193

of business is *not* making mortgage loans. Bank rates are competitive by each bank can only offer its own rates.

Your bank may offer a discount or incentive on your loan if you maintain a checking or savings account at that institution.

Credit Unions

These institutions are regularly under attack by lending competitors because credit unions do not pay federal taxes and enjoy certain taxable advantages that other lending institutions do not. They are formed by a group of individuals with a common interest such as state government and community education employees or religious groups.

Savings & Loan Associations

Savings and loans accept deposits from customers into savings / money market accounts and pay interest on those accounts. To prevent a relapse like the S&L crisis in the 1980s, President Bush in 1989 signed the Financial Institutions Reform, Recovery, and Enforcement Act of 1989 (FIRREA). Many savings and loans are now regulated by the Department of U. S. Treasury, Office of Thrift Supervision. Primary source of business is making real estate loans. Savings and loans do not make business or commercial loans but lend for construction, purchase or home improvement purposes. The process for obtaining a mortgage is a bit easier than going to a commercial bank.

Customers must meet qualifications to be eligible for membership. Interest rates and terms are typically very attractive and competitive. Many credit unions do not sell their mortgage loans on the secondary market.

Private Individual

Anybody with money in the bank can make a real estate loan to you as long as they comply with federal and state regulations regarding such items as interest rates, fees and charges, and provide legally required disclosures. The seller can carry back common financing instruments such as a mortgage, trust deed or land contract. No appraisal or title policy may be required, but you should still obtain an appraisal and title protection.

Owner financing works best on properties that are free and clear because an existing loan will most likely contain an alienation clause.

Stock Brokerages & Online Lenders

You might be astonished to learn that the company handling your IRAs or mutual funds or online savings also makes mortgage loans. A few easily recognizable names are INGDirect, Charles Schwab, and Ditech.

If you need to shake hands with your loan officer in person, an online lender might not be for you. Internet lenders seem to work best for sophisticated borrowers with great FICO scores who know exactly what they want. Contact only reputable and known companies with secure sites, and stay away from fly-by-night operators.

(An IRA is an Individual Retirement Account, (Private Pension) and provides either a tax-deferred or tax-free way of saving for retirement. There are many different types of accounts within the world of IRAs, depending on the financial goals and situations of each individual, though traditional and Roth IRAs are the most common choices. A traditional IRA allows tax-deductible contributions of up to $4,000 per year, or more if you are over age 50. Choosing IRAs can be

complicated, depending on the financial situation and may require the services of a certified financial planner.)

Energy Efficient Mortgages

"Energy Efficient Mortgages," also known as EEMs, make it easier for borrowers to qualify for loans to purchase homes with specific energy-efficiency improvements. Lenders can offer conventional EEMs, FHA EEMs, or VA EEMs. Conventional EEMs can be offered by lenders who sell their loans to Fannie Mae and Freddie Mac. Conventional EEMs increase the purchasing power of buying an energy efficient home by allowing the lender to increase the borrower's income by a dollar amount equal to the estimated energy savings. The Fannie Mae loan also adjusts the value of the home to reflect the value of the energy efficiency measures. FHA EEMs allow lenders to add 100 percent of the additional cost of cost-effective energy efficiency improvements to an already approved mortgage loan (as long as the additional costs do not exceed $4000 or 5 percent of the value of the home, up to a maximum of $8000, whichever is greater). No additional down payment is required, and the FHA loan limits won't interfere with the process of obtaining the EEM. FHA EEMs are available for site-built as well as for manufactured homes.

The Mortgage Offer

You will get a written mortgage offer from your mortgage broker. You should allow two – four weeks from the date of your application to receiving a written mortgage offer; it can take longer as getting information required is not easy to come by. Your lender may get written references from your employer and bank (or accountant if you're self-employed) and your current lender or landlord. They'll also run credit checks to make sure you've paid off your debts in the past.

Once you receive the offer you will generally have 28 days from receipt of the offer in which to accept it, after which time it will lapse. You can of course reapply and if it's done within 6 months, you will not be subject to any fees. The mortgage offer usually requires you to take out buildings insurance, in case something happens to the property before you've paid off the mortgage. Read the offer and make sure you understand any early redemption penalties.

Choose a solicitor or licensed conveyance

You'll need someone to carry out the legal side of things - local searches, drawing up contracts and other legal paperwork. You could use a conveyance solicitor or a licensed conveyance - or even do part of it yourself (but make sure you know exactly what you're taking on). Some lenders have preferred solicitors, or you may be able to get a personal recommendation. You can also search online or in the phone book. (The lender will insist on a professional conveyance to carry out the valuation.)

Property valuation

Your lender will usually have the property valued to make sure it's worth the price you've agreed to pay. If it's not, it could affect how much they'll lend you. It's advisable to get your own survey done too or to upgrade the lender's valuation survey to a more detailed one.

Exchange and completion

If you're buying, once you've got a formal mortgage offer, your solicitor can agree a date for exchanging contracts with the seller's solicitor. At this time you usually pay a percentage of the purchase price as a non-refundable deposit and commit to paying the rest on the agreed completion date (when the property becomes yours).

Who Should Own the Property? (In who's name?)

There are many ways of structuring the purchase of a home in the United States. Each method has a significant possible advantage and disadvantage. It may not be important now, but in the future it could save you, your spouse or your children thousands of dollars. Some states will force you to give part of your estate to your surviving spouse. If you have children from previous marriages this is very important.

Think about it, you marry and have children and build up some wealth, your spouse dies, a few years later you remarry, your new spouse has children from a previous relationship. When you die now, do you want your estate to go to your new spouse and their children? Get it done legally. A prenuptial agreement is a good idea, it's not very romantic, but a marriage is a legally binding contract under law. Get it right from the start. Look at ex-Beatle Paul McCartney. His latest marriage of less than 3 years cost him over $750 million? For over 40 years he has worked hard writing, performing and producing music, his new Ex-wife wiped out half of that work in one go.

Sole Ownership

In some case it may be an advantage to put the property in the name of one person only. Some reasons could be age, if you are a (Lucky) 85 year old man and your partner is a 21 year old it would make sense. Or if you are self-employed in a high risk business, you may find it safer to put the home in your partner's name. (In Florida and if you are made bankrupt by business debt, that can't take your home from you, your home is protected.) Also if you are a single person, Sole ownership is for you.

Joint Ownership

This should be used as a general guide only - if you require legal advice you should consult an attorney. Joint ownership refers to two parties owning property together. Property in this sense may apply to a residence, a business, or intellectual property like patents. Joint ownership can be beneficial if one partner dies, as property does not have to go through probate. It can also be problematic, particularly in the area of intellectual property, or property jointly owned by a parent and a child. Joint ownership is most often applied in the real estate market, where it refers to two people who jointly own a home. In most cases, these two people are a married couple. This type of joint ownership can reduce hassle. It is not necessary for a person to wait for probate in order to own the whole house if his or her spouse dies. When a spouse dies, it may be necessary to restructure finances immediately. Being able to completely own one's home immediately assures an easy transfer of assets. Additionally, in many states, a house owned by a married couple, where one partner dies, is not considered an addition of property to the surviving owner, so no taxes are assessed to sole ownership.

Joint ownership can also simplify division of assets in a divorce. Anything that is owned jointly is split. One person can chose to buy out the other's person's half, but it is very difficult to contest rights to property when it is jointly owned. Couples may barter their ownership status for access to other portions of the estate, but at least a property that is jointly owned eliminates arguments about the extent to which each partner is entitled to the property.

Joint ownership of property is not limited to spouses. A parent can decide to jointly own his or her house with a child. When the child is financially stable and an only child, this may make good sense, since that child will not require probate to inherit the house. Most realtors and financial advisors, however, caution against joint ownership with a child.

Several concerns come to light immediately. If a parent has joint ownership of a house with one child and there are other siblings, the parent may request that the proceeds of the house be evenly divided between siblings upon the parent's death. Joint ownership overrides the obligation for the child who jointly owns the house to honor this request. Since parent and child jointly own the house, the house immediately passes to the surviving owner upon the parent's death. Other siblings may never receive whatever entitlements to the house their parents might have desired for them.

Joint ownership can also cause problems if the financial prospects of the child are unstable. If, for example, the child enters bankruptcy or owes back taxes, a parent can lose his or her home when creditors collect owed funds. If the child is uninsured and hospitalized, the same can occur. The child's future in regards to the house is also at issue if the parent becomes seriously ill or is at financial risk.

Joint ownership of businesses or intellectual property implies certain rights to both parties, and as such may require extensive drafting of legal documents to avoid pitfalls. For example, if a patent is jointly owned, either partner may sell the patent, permit the use of the patent, or release information about the patent without the agreement of the other partner. This violates the whole concept of a patent, in many respects, since the goal of a patent is to keep other manufacturers from producing the same product. To protect both partners, it is necessary to draw up binding legal agreements that prohibit this and other behaviors that could reduce the profitability of the patent.

Further, once one partner dies, the other partner fully owns the patent. The deceased partner's family has no right to inherit any profits associated with the patent after the partner's death, because the profits do not belong to them. To reduce these risks, partners may want to consider alternative methods of owning a patent with which inheritance to other family members is ensured.

Ownership of property, other methods.

It is possible to have your IRA own the property; it is also possible start a corporation (Limited company) and own a property via the company. This way as a director, you own shares in the company and you do not own the home. *Why?* Tax savings is one, another is protection. If someone sues you and attempts to take you to the cleaners, they can't touch the property it's owned by the company. They can however take part of the company unless you have a family limited liability trust set up. See an attorney; it has to be set correct.

The main reason property owners in The United States, myself included have property in corporations is for tax reason. If you have some investment properties, these can be owned by the company, the company then protects you. Let's say you have a tenant that sues you because you have mold in the home and they now have lung cancer. Yes, they can sue the company and possibly bankrupt it, but as you don't own the home, they can't touch you. As for tax, all expenses including your wage as property manager is a business expense. This includes travel back and forth to the properties. I own properties in various States. I don't as I use property managers, but could travel across the country to inspect them all as a business expense.

Home Owners Associations (HOA)

In the United States many subdivisions, streets, blocks and areas, are controlled by an HOA. In theory they are great, they control deed restrictions etc. A homeowners' association (abbrev. HOA) is the legal entity created by a real estate developer for the purpose of developing, managing and selling a community of homes. It is given the authority to enforce the covenants, conditions, and restrictions (CC&Rs) and to manage the common amenities of the development. It allows the developer to legally exit responsibility of the community typically by transferring ownership of the association to the homeowners after selling off a predetermined number of lots. Most homeowners' associations are non-profit corporations, and are subject to state statutes that govern non-profit corporations and homeowners' associations.

The fastest growing form of housing in the United States today is common-interest developments, a category that includes planned-unit developments of single-family homes, condominiums, and cooperative apartments.[] Since 1964, homeowners' associations have become increasingly common in the USA. The Community Associations Institute trade association estimated that HOAs governed 23 million American homes and 57 million residents in 2007. A homeowners' association is incorporated by the developer prior to the initial sale of homes, and the Covenants, Conditions, and Restrictions (CC&Rs) are recorded when the property is subdivided. When a homeowner purchases a home governed by an HOA, the CC&Rs are included with the deed.

Powers

Like a city, associations provide services, regulate activities, levy assessments, and impose fines. Unlike a municipal government, homeowner association governance is not subject to the Constitutional constraints that public government must abide by. Some of the tasks which HOAs carry out would otherwise be performed by local governments. A homeowners' association can enforce its actions through private legal action under civil law; and unlike any other private organization, homeowners' associations have the power to fine its residents, which is considered a government or police power.

Association boards appoint corporate officers, and may create subcommittees, such as "architectural control committees," pool committees and neighborhood watch committees. Association boards are comprised of volunteers from the community who are elected by owners at the annual meeting to represent the association and make decisions for all homeowners

Assessments

Homeowner associations can compel homeowners to pay a share of common expenses, usually per-unit or based on square footage. These expenses generally arise from common property, which varies dramatically depending on the type of association. Some associations are, quite literally, towns, complete with private roads, services, utilities, amenities, community buildings, pools, and even schools. Many condominium associations consider the roofs and exteriors of the structures as the responsibility of the association. Other associations have no common property, but may charge for services or other matters. Assessments paid to homeowner associations in the United States amount to billions of dollars a year.

Benefits

The purpose of a homeowners association is to maintain, enhance and protect the common areas and interests of an association (also called a subdivision or neighborhood). This can allow an individual homeowner access to an amenity (pond, pool, clubhouse, etc.) that he may not be able to afford on his own. Each member of a homeowners association pays assessments. The assessments are used to pay the expenses of community. Some examples are entrance monuments, landscaping for the common area, amenities like clubhouses, tennis courts, or walking trails, insurance for commonly-owned structures and areas, mailing costs for newsletters or other correspondence, a management company or on-site manager, or any other item delineated in the governing documents or agreed to by the Board of Directors. A board of directors can be sued if it breeches its duties, but board members risk nothing financially in these suits. Association insurance provides not only for a board member's legal expense, but any judgment attained against them.

Power of the HOA

In some U.S. states, including California, and Texas, a homeowners association can foreclose a member's house without any judicial procedure in order to collect special assessments, fees and fines. Other states, like Florida, require a judicial hearing. Foreclosure without a judicial hearing can occur when a power of sale clause exists in a mortgage or deed of trust. Most HOA's spend their time informing homeowners to cut the grass, weed areas, repaint house, etc.

The type of power they have depends on the deed restrictions. Some homeowners hate it and try to rebel, (But in up in court) They feel they can cut the grass when they want, and paint the house any color they want, plus leave a boat out on the front driveway. If you are like that, don't move into a deed restricted area. A deed restricted community home is far more valuable than non deed restricted. This is due to the fact the homes are kept tidy and gardens are all immaculate.

When you walk down a street that is deed restricted in some cases, you will see NO for sale signs, No trucks, boats, bikes left on driveways. The grass will be green, weed free and cut. You will not find bright blue or bright pink homes; they will not have football stickers and posters in the windows. The trash cans are all put away and not visible, you will not see satellite dishes or solar panels on the roof. (They may have these, but will be at the back of the houses) Driveways will not have oil spills on them. Plus you will not see hundreds of tacky plastic *made in China* garden statues. Its sounds harsh but the homes look great. The homeowners normally pay to get the grass cut and yards weeded weekly, many get a discount as the grass cutters can do many homes at once. If they want to paint the home of make alterations, they can, but just have to submit an application in first. It's the other homeowners who sit on the board of the HOA. So anything you do to improve your home they are for as it will enhance the street and increase all home values.

I Live in a deed restricted area and have for many years been on the board of the HOA. It actually brings the community together, street parties, Easter egg hunt for children, at Halloween; the homes are decorated with pumpkins and witches. The children from the street play trick or treat. At Christmas time (Normally the day after thanksgiving, the last Thursday of November) the street is decorated for Christmas. In the United States they really do decorate the homes. If you have seen the films "National lampoons Christmas", or "Christmas with the Kranks" this is what it is really like. I moved from the United Kingdom to Sunny Florida. It seems strange putting Christmas lights on Palm trees and Orange & Grapefruit trees with fruit on them, but its looks great at night.

Christmas homes in the United States *circa 2008*

Choosing the Location of your property.

If you have been reading page by page you will have already learned that if you have children and you want them to go to a particular public school, you have to live in certain zip codes for each school. You can get this information by calling the school or sometimes on the schools website.

You will also need to decide what sort of home you want, house, apt or condominium. Do you want to live in a deed restricted area or not. I would recommend that you live in an area for the very least 3-6 months. Rent a property and take your time, drive at different times of the day. It may be quite on a Monday at 10am, but at 4pm when the local children are out, take a look and see if this is the area you want your family to live. Again go back at 7.30 pm, and at the weekends, this will show you how many cars are in the area and the availability of parking. Do you want to live in a big city, like New York or Chicago? The concept of "moving to the big city" is so well-ingrained in the American mythology that it's practically beyond dispute. It's virtually assumed that those young people with the opportunity to do so will move promptly upon graduation (usually from college) to the largest city that will take them. Going to work and live in smaller communities is looked upon as a social misstep -- in some cases, a virtual declaration that one is incapable of success amid the challenges of the big city.

But what if it is a rational choice?

The one factor that most people identify as the deciding appeal of large metropolitan areas is that, by living there, one can be "close to the action." And, geographically, there's no dispute. Living in Chicago, for instance, places one much closer to the major cultural opportunities that the city has to offer than, for instance, living in Des Moines.

But, as anyone who has ever traveled within a large city knows, geographic "closeness" isn't the same as a quick trip. In fact, just two significant factors are enough to make it evident that it's a perfectly rational decision to live in a much smaller metropolitan area, even if one wants to be close to the action.

Factor One: Time Spent in Transit

Consider Chicago versus Des Moines. The average (probably mean) one-way commute in Chicago is 31 minutes per day, while in Des Moines it's about 19.

Chicago	Des Moines	Difference
One-Way Commute (min)	31	19	12
Round-Trip Per Day (min)	62	38	24
Round-Trip Per Week (min)	310	190	120
Round-Trip Per 50-Week Work Year (min)	15,500	9,500	6,000

That's 6,000 minutes per year that the average commuter in Chicago spends in-transit that the average Des Moines commuter doesn't. A difference of 100 hours each year.

A drive between downtown Chicago and the far-western suburbs of Des Moines takes about five to five-and-a-half hours. We'll round up and call it an 11-hour round trip. For the difference in commuting times, the average Des Moines commuter could travel to Chicago nine times a year. Realistically, can most Chicago residents say that they take advantage of nine cultural opportunities a year that are exclusive to Chicago itself? Nine opportunities each year they could not have experienced in Des Moines, or Cedar Rapids, or Madison, or any other medium-sized metropolitan area within a reasonable driving radius of Chicago? Likely not.

This effect, by the way, is compounded in a number of ways, to the advantage of the smaller communities. For those who live in the suburbs, commuting times generally grow much worse in the major cities; meantime, many of the good jobs in the smaller metros are located in office parks that are often located in those same suburbs. It's not uncommon to find suburban Des Moines residents living just five minutes from the workplace. The suburb-to-suburb commute in Chicago is often as bad as or worse than the suburb-to-city commute.

Simultaneously, commute times don't account for the additional time spent in transit between home and chores or leisure travel. Accounting for the additional time inevitably spent en route to the grocery store, the gym, church, or even the gas station is likely to make the case even stronger for smaller metropolitan areas.

Factor Two: Cost of Living

the cost of living in major metropolitan areas is substantially higher than in many smaller communities. The median home price in metropolitan Chicago, for instance, is nearly twice what it is in Des Moines. Overall, Chicago's cost-of-living index is more than one-third above the national average, while Des Moines is about 10% lower than the average. Median household incomes for the two communities are not substantially different -- $50,538 in Des Moines; $52,121 in Chicago.

The result? One can live in relatively greater comfort in the smaller metropolitan area than in the larger one. And with the extra disposable income, one can afford to make an occasional trip from Des Moines to Chicago in order to take in those much-vaunted cultural attractions.

The Bottom Line: There's a Very Rational Argument for Living in Smaller Metros

The bottom line is that the patronizing attitude many people put on about their peers who choose to live outside the biggest metropolitan areas is nothing more than that -- an attitude, and an unsubstantiated one at that. Certainly, some people will choose to live in smaller communities simply because they are anxious about moving to the larger cities. But that doesn't negate the rationality of the choice many others make to live in smaller metropolitan areas. It's not necessarily the parochial choice some make it out to be. In fact, based on the additional leisure time available and the substantially lower cost of living, smaller metropolitan areas may be the ideal hometowns of choice for people who want to maximize their opportunities to travel and engage in other cosmopolitan pursuits -- ones that their peers living in larger cities can neither afford nor spare the time to enjoy.

Property Tax

Property tax, millage tax is an ad valorem tax that an owner of real estate or other property pays on the value of the property being taxed. This is levied annually on property owners in all states to help pay for local services such as primary and secondary education, Police, Fire and Ambulance services, libraries, public transport, waste disposal and highways. There are three species or types of property: Land, Improvements to Land (immovable man made things), and personally (movable man made things). Real estate, real property or realty are all terms for the combination of land and improvements. The taxing authority requires and/or performs an appraisal of the monetary value of the property, and tax is assessed in proportion to that value. Forms of property tax used vary between countries and jurisdictions.

There is a form of tax which is often confused with the property tax. This is the special assessment tax. These are two distinct forms of taxation: one (ad valorem tax) relying upon the fair market value of the property being taxed for justification, and the other, (special assessment) relying upon a special enhancement called a "benefit" for its justification.

The property tax rate is often given as a percentage (amount of tax per hundred currency units of property value). It may also be expressed as a per mill (amount of tax per thousand currency units of property value), which is also known as a millage rate or mill levy. (A mill is also one-thousandth of a dollar.) To calculate the property tax, the authority will multiply the assessed value of the property by the mill rate and then divide by 1,000. For example, a property with an assessed value of US$ 50,000 located in a municipality with a mill rate of 20 mills would have a property tax bill of US$ 1,000.00 per year.

In the United States, property tax on real estate is usually assessed by local government, at the municipal or county level. A very important benefit of a tax on property over a tax on income is that the revenue always equals the tax levy, unlike income or sales taxes, which can result in shortfalls producing deficits. The property tax always produces the required revenue for municipalities' tax levies. On the other hand property taxes can have a negative impact on individuals with fixed incomes such as the elderly and those who have lost their jobs. Gentrification in low income areas of a city can drive property taxes to the point where long time residents of an area are forced to leave.

The assessment is made up of two components — the improvement or building value and the land or site value. In some states, personal property is also taxed. A tax assessor is a public official who determines the value of real property for the purpose of apportioning the tax levy. An appraiser may work for government or private industry and may determine the value of real property for any purpose.

Tax assessor offices maintain inventory information about improvements to real estate. They also create and maintain tax maps. This is accomplished with the help of surveyors. On tax maps, individual properties are shown and given unique parcel identifiers. The tax maps help to ensure that no properties are omitted from the tax rolls and that no properties are taxed more than once. Real property taxes are usually collected by an official other than the assessor. Duplicate examples of a proposed alternate to ad valorum assessments is provided at the following sites as sponsored by the Henry George Foundation. Maryland, King County, Washington, Indiana, New Jersey, New York. In fact many localities have gone online.

The assessment of an individual piece of real estate may be according to one or more of the normally accepted methods of valuation (i.e. income approach, market value or replacement cost). Assessments may be given at 100 percent of value or at some lesser percentage. In most if not all assessment jurisdictions, the determination of value made by the assessor is subject to some sort of administrative or judicial review, if the appeal is instituted by the property owner.

Ad valorem (of value) property taxes are based on fair market property values of individual estates. A local tax assessor then applies an established assessment rate to the fair market value. By multiplying the tax rate x against the assessed value of the property, a tax due is calculated. These taxes are collected by municipalities such as cities, counties, and districts in many locations in the United States. They fund municipal budgets for school systems, sewers, parks, libraries, fire stations, hospitals, etc.. Relatively recently, US property tax rates increased well above similar rates in other "non-communists" countries, and exceeded 5% in some US states, thus becoming the main dwelling expense after construction. This is a results of the specific US situation, where the US federal government collects high personal income tax (very high as compare to taxes applied for federal purposes in other countries) and uses it, while US states and localities have to find other ways to collect funds to support at least some level of local infrastructure, including roads and bridges, school and college education, low reinforcement, public safety and healthcare and so on.

After determining a budget at the municipal level, a legislative appropriation determines how the monies will be collected and distributed. After that, a tax authority levies the tax. An appeal is permitted. Equalization is then considered by a board of equalizers to assure fair treatment. Then a tax rate is determined by dividing the municipal budget by the assessment role of that municipality. Multiplying tax rate by the assessed value of one's property determines one's tax rate.

Some jurisdictions have both ad valorem and non-ad valorem property taxes (better known as special assessments). The latter come in the form of a fixed charge (regardless of the value of the underlying property) for items such as street lighting and storm sewer control.

In the United States, another form of *property tax* is the *personal property tax*, which can target

Automobiles, boats, aircraft and other vehicles;

Other valuable durable goods such as works of art (most household goods and personal effects are usually exempt);

Business inventory;

Intangible assets such as stocks and bonds.

In some states, it is permissible to separate the real estate tax, into two separate taxes—one the land value and one on the building value.

Personal property taxes can be assessed at almost any level of government, though they are perhaps most commonly assessed by states

In the absence of comprehensive urban planning policies, property tax on real estate changes the incentives for developing land, which in turn affects land use patterns. One of the main concerns is whether or not it encourages urban sprawl.

The market value of undeveloped real estate reflects a property's current use as well as its development potential.

As a city expands, relatively cheap and undeveloped lands (such as farms, ranches, private conservation parks, etc.) increase in value as neighboring areas are developed into retail, industrial, or residential units. This raises the land value, which increases the property tax that must be paid on agricultural land, but does not increase the amount of revenue per land area available to the owner. This, along with a higher sale price, increases the incentive to rent or sell agricultural land to developers. On the other hand, a property owner who develops a parcel must thereafter pay a higher tax, based on the value of the improvements. This makes the development less attractive than it would otherwise be. Overall, these effects result in lower density development, which tends to increase sprawl.

Attempts to reduce the impact of property taxes on sprawl include:

Land value taxation - This method separates the value of a given property into its actual components - land value and improvement value. A gradually lower and lower tax is levied on the improvement value and a higher tax is levied on the land value to insure revenue-neutrality. This method is also known as two-tiered or split-rate taxation.

Most cities have a higher building tax than surrounding suburban and rural areas. By removing improvements as a factor in the property taxes, the penalty against construction and renovation in already urbanized areas is removed. Increasing the tax on land value discourages land speculation - which forces development further away from central cities - and encourages efficient land use.

Current-use valuation - This method assesses the value of a given property based only upon its current use. Much like land value taxation, this reduces the effect of city encroachment.

Conservation easements - The property owner adds a restriction to the property prohibiting future development. This effectively removes the development potential as a factor in the property taxes.

Exemptions - Exempting favored classes of real estate (such as farms, ranches, cemeteries or private conservation parks) from the property tax altogether or assessing their value at a very minimal amount (for example, $1 per acre).

Forcing higher density housing - In the Portland, Oregon area (for example), local municipalities are often forced to accept higher density housing with small lot sizes. This is governed by a multi-county development control board, in Portland's case Metro.

Urban growth boundary or Green belt - Government declares some land undevelopable until a date in the future. This forces regional development back into the urban core, increasing density but also land and housing prices. It may also cause development to skip over the restricted-use zone, to occur in more distant areas, or to move to other cities. As property increases in value the possibility exists that new buyers might pay taxes on outdated values thus placing an unfair burden on the rest of the property owners. To correct this imbalance municipalities periodically revalue property. Revaluation produces an up to date value to be used in determination of the tax rate necessary to produce the required tax levy.

A consequence of this is that existing owners are reassessed as well as new owners and thus are required to pay taxes on property the value of which is determined by market forces.

In an effort to relieve the frequently large tax burdens on existing owner's communities have introduced exemptions.

In some states, laws provide for exemptions (typically called homestead exemptions) and/or limits on the percentage increase in tax, which limit the yearly increase in property tax so that owner-occupants are not "taxed out of their homes". Generally, these exemptions and ceilings are available only to property owners who use their property as their principal residence. Homestead exemptions generally cannot be claimed on investment properties and second homes. When a homesteaded property changes ownership, the property tax often rises sharply and the property's sale price may become the basis for new exemptions and limits available to the new owner-occupant.

Homestead exemptions increase the complexity of property tax collection and sometimes provide an easy opportunity for people who own several properties to benefit from tax credits to which they are not entitled. Since there is no national database that links home ownership with Social Security numbers, landlords sometimes gain homestead tax credits by claiming multiple properties in different states, and even their own state, as their "principal residence", while only one property is truly their residence. In 2005, several US Senators and Congressmen were found to have erroneously claimed "second homes" in the greater Washington, D.C. area as their "principal residences", giving them property tax credits to which they were not entitled.

Undeserved homestead exemption credits became so ubiquitous in the state of Maryland that a law was passed in the 2007 legislative session to require validation of principal residence status through the use of a social security number matching system. The bill passed unanimously in the

Maryland House of Delegates and Senate and was signed into law by the Governor.

The fairness of property tax collection and distribution is a hotly-debated topic. Some people feel school systems would be more uniform if the taxes were collected and distributed at a state level, thereby equalizing the funding of school districts. Others are reluctant to have a higher level of government determine the rates and allocations, preferring to leave the decisions to government levels "closer to the people".

In Rhode Island efforts are being made to modify revaluation practices to preserve the major benefit of property taxation, the reliability of tax revenue, while providing for what some view as a correction of the unfair distribution of tax burdens on existing owners of property.

The Supreme Court has held that Congress cannot directly tax land ownership, unless the tax is apportioned among the states based upon representation/population. In an apportioned land tax, each state would have its own rate of taxation sufficient to raise it pro-rata share of the total revenue to be financed by a land tax. Such an apportioned tax on land had been used on many occasions up through the Civil War.

Indirect taxes on the transfer of land are permitted without apportionment: in the past, this has taken the form of requiring revenue stamps to be affixed to deeds and mortgages, but these are no longer required by federal law. Under the Internal Revenue Code, the government realizes a substantial amount of revenue from income taxes on capital gains from the sale of land, and in estate taxes from the passage of property (including land) upon the death of its owner.

The Supreme Court has not directly ruled on the question of whether Congress may impose an un-apportioned tax on the "privilege" of owning land with the "measure" of the tax being the value of the land.

Appeal against property tax.

You can appeal against your property assessment, which may cut your bill by as much as 20%. Check your property record card at your local assessor's office.

The following terms and definitions are provided to help you understand how your property is valued and assessed.

Real Market Value (RMV) is the value the assessor has estimated your property would sell for on the open market as of the assessment date. RMV appears on most property tax statements.

Maximum Assessed Value (MAV) is the greatest of 103 percent of the prior year's assessed value or 100 percent of the prior year's MAV. MAV is not limited to an increase of 3 percent if certain changes are made to your property. These changes are called exceptions. MAV does not appear on most tax statements.

Assessed Value (AV) is the value used to calculate your tax. It is the lesser of RMV or MAV. Assessed value appears on your tax statement.

Exception means a change to property, not including general ongoing maintenance and repair or minor construction. Changes that could affect maximum assessed value include new construction or additions, major remodeling or reconstruction, rezoning with use consistent with the change in zoning, a partition or subdivision, or a disqualification from special assessment or exemption. Minor construction is defined as additions of real property improvements with a real market value that does not exceed $10,000 in one assessment year or $25,000 over a period of five assessment years. Exception value does not appear on your tax statement.

Specially Assessed Value (SAV) is a value established by statute. The legislature has created several programs that set lower assessed value levels for certain types of property. Each program has specific applications and use requirements. Examples of property that may qualify for special assessment are farmland, forestland, historic property, government-restricted low income multi-unit housing, and property that qualify as "open space." SAV appears on most tax statements for property that is specially assessed.

The majority of appeals will be based on a difference of opinion between you and the assessor about RMV. In such cases, you will need to present evidence about the market value of your property as it existed on the assessment date. Evidence might include an appraisal report of your property done by an independent appraiser or a comparison of your property with similar properties that have recently sold in your area.

Comparing the value on the tax roll of your house to the value on the tax roll of your neighbor's house, or comparing the taxes you pay to the taxes your neighbor pays is generally not considered satisfactory evidence.

The following are examples in which an appeal of RMV may result in a tax benefit:

The board reduces the RMV below the assessed value currently on the roll.

Your property has recently been improved and the board reduces the value of the new construction.

The board reduces the RMV of your property, and the reduction requires property taxes to be reduced to meet constitutional limits on the education and general government categories of your taxes. You must file appeals between the date the tax statements are mailed and December 31. If December 31 falls on a Saturday, Sunday, or legal holiday, the filing deadline moves to the next business day. File your petition with the county clerk's office in the county where the property is located. You can get the forms you need from your county clerk or county assessor's office. Please note if you are on a visa and not a green card you will not get any local State exemptions.

Section 30) The Importance of Making a Will and Estate Planning.

If you move to the United States, I hope this will not be required for a long time, but it's one thing in life we are certain of; we are all going to die. A *will* is a legal document, drafted and executed in accordance with state law, which becomes irrevocable at your death. In your will, you can name:

Your beneficiaries. These are family members, friends, a domestic partner, or charitable organizations who will receive your assets as you direct. You may provide for specific gifts of such items as jewelry or a specific sum of money to named beneficiaries. You should also provide for the distribution of the *residue* of your estate - that is, your remaining assets (they do not need to be specified) which are not specifically given to individuals or organizations in your will.

A guardian for your minor children. You may nominate a person who will have the responsibility to care for your child if you and your spouse die before the child attains 18 years of age. You may also name a guardian - who may or may not be the same person - to be responsible for management of assets given to a minor child, until the child attains 18 years of age.

An executor. This person or institution of your choice, named in your will and appointed by the probate court, collects and manages your assets, pays your debts and expenses and any taxes that might be due, and then, in a manner approved by the court, distributes your assets to your beneficiaries in accordance with the provisions of your will. Your executor plays a very important role with significant responsibilities.

It can be a time-consuming job. You should choose your executor carefully. A will is a part of your "estate plan." Generally speaking, your will affects only those assets which are in your name alone at your death. Some assets which are not affected by your will include:

Life insurance. The cash proceeds from an insurance policy on your life are paid to whomever you have designated as beneficiary of the policy in a form filed with the insurance company Ñ no matter who the beneficiaries under your will may be.

Retirement plans. Assets held in retirement plans, such as a 401(k) or an IRA, are transferred to whomever you have named as beneficiary in the plan documents.

Assets owned as a joint tenant. Assets such as real estate, automobiles, bank accounts and other property held in joint tenancy will pass to the surviving joint tenant upon your death, not in accordance with any directions in your will.

"Transfer on death" or "pay on death." Securities and brokerage accounts may be registered or held with beneficiaries named on the security or account. Title is held in the name of the owner and the names of the beneficiaries are preceded by the words "transfer on death" or "TOD." Other assets, such as bank accounts and U.S. savings bonds, may be held in a similar form using the owner's name and the beneficiaries' names preceded by the words "paid on death" or "POD."

"Community property with right of survivorship." Married couples or registered domestic partners may hold title to their community property in their names as "community property with right of survivorship." Property held in that manner at the death of the first spouse or domestic partner is not affected by that spouse's will, but passes instead to the surviving spouse or domestic partner.

Living trusts. Assets held in a *revocable living trust* at your death are distributed pursuant to the provisions of that trust document. A living trust allows for the management of your assets during your lifetime and the transfer of those assets pursuant to the terms of the trust without a court-supervised probate proceeding.

Your spouse's or domestic partner's half of community property. In California, any assets acquired by you and your spouse or registered domestic partner from earnings during your marriage or domestic partnership are community property.

You and your spouse or registered domestic partner own equal shares of those assets. Your will, therefore, affects only your half of the community property, not your spouse's or domestic partner's.

Assets that either of you owned at the date of the marriage or registered domestic partnership, together with gifts and inheritances given to just one of you during the marriage or domestic partnership, are that individual's separate property. Your will affects all of your separate property held in your name alone.

Even if your entire estate consists of property held in joint tenancy, a life insurance policy and a retirement plan, you should still consider making a will.

If the other joint tenant dies before you do, then the property held in joint tenancy will be in your name alone and subject to your will. If named beneficiaries die before you do, the assets subject to a beneficiary designation may be payable to your estate.

You may unexpectedly be entitled to a bonus, a prize, a refund, or may receive an unexpected inheritance which would then be subject to your will as well. If you have minor children, the nomination of a guardian of their person and estate is a very important reason for making a will.

What Happens If I Don't Have a Will?

If you are married or have established a registered domestic partnership, your spouse or domestic partner will receive all of your community property. Your spouse or domestic partner also will receive part of your separate property, and the rest of your separate property will be distributed to your children or grandchildren, parents, sisters, brothers, nieces, nephews or other close relatives.

If you are not married or in a registered domestic partnership, your assets will be distributed to your children or grandchildren, if you have any - or to your parents, sisters, brothers, nieces, nephews or other relatives.

If your spouse or domestic partner died before you, his or her relatives may also be entitled to some or all of your estate. Friends, a non-registered domestic partner or your favorite charities will receive nothing if you die without a will.

The State in which you live is the beneficiary of your estate if you die intestate and you (and your deceased spouse or domestic partner) has no living relatives.

You can buy a 'Fill in the blanks' forms on line, if you use this type (It's normally better than nothing) ensure you get one that's for your State as each State will have different laws.

Section 31) Eating Out.

The United States is not really noted for its cuisine; many from outside the U.S think the Americans live on Peanut butter and Jelly sandwiches plus burgers. America also has an image of fat people. However you could not be further from the truth. The UK is the Worlds' Fattest country; it has more overweight people per capita than any other country. It is true, The US does have some 'couch breakers' but on average, Americans are not fat.

America has the best food in the world. No other country can come close. In most cities there is a multitude of eating places. Yes it has MacDonald's, Burger Kings, KFC and Subway etc on most streets, but so does Europe now.

In New York there are over 63,000 eating places, over 25,000 of these are in the city of New York. In the city that's an eating place for every 300 residents. In San Francisco CA there is one restaurant for every inhabitant. Before Hurricane Katrina, New Orleans was the same.

America's restaurants are the cornerstones of the nation's economy, providing career opportunities for more Americans than any other private sector employer. Our industry includes more than 947,000 restaurant and foodservice outlets and 12.9 million people. A majority of the industry is made up of small business owners who embody the spirit of entrepreneurship in America today. Many are franchises and it may be your choice to buy a restaurant for your visa, you will find the strict health and safety rules hard to handle, food hygiene is critical.

American Cattle

American beef feeds the families of the world...and it all begins on the farm. The beef you cook at home or order in a restaurant comes from cattle that spend the vast majority of their lives grazing in fields on family-owned farms and ranches around the country.

There are about 800,000 cattle producers across the country who are dedicated to caring for their herds and producing safe, wholesome beef. For most beef producers, raising cattle is a family tradition passed down through generations.

Cattle farmers and ranchers are an important foundation of American values and they are proud of what they do. Beef producers spend most of their days taking care of their animals and the land because it's the right thing to do and because it's the only way they can sustain their way of life for future generations. Cattle and beef production represent the largest single segment of American agriculture. In fact, the U.S. Department of Agriculture (USDA) says more farms are classified as beef cattle operations (35%) than any other type of farm. Most farms and ranches in the United States, including cattle ranches, are family owned and operated, but cattle operations have long been considered multi-generational endeavors. An Iowa survey of cattle producers showed that 60 percent of producers in that state alone expect to pass their operation on to their children.

There are about 800,000 beef producers in the United States, who are responsible for nearly 100 million head of beef cattle. According to USDA, producers of meat animals in 2005 were responsible for more than $64 billion in added value to the U.S. economy, as measured by their contribution to the national output. Family farmers and ranchers have finished cattle on grain for more than 100 years. Cattle feeding became more prevalent after World War I and through the Great Depression, but were not fully developed on a commercial scale until after World War II, when grain was plentiful, the economy was robust and consumers demanded tender, great tasting beef that was available year-round.

U.S. grain-fed beef has earned a worldwide reputation for its quality, consistency and taste. It has tenderness and a rich flavor that taste tests show are important to consumers. In fact, consumers will go out of their way to select beef cuts with these grain-fed characteristics.

If you have not tried a fresh Steak in the U.S, You have not yet eaten steak. Buffalo steak is available at certain restaurants, it's very low in fat, cholesterol and the flavor is the next grade up from beef Steak. You have to try it.

US Pork

The pork industry is constantly changing and U.S. pork producers will adapt in order to continue producing safe, wholesome pork for consumers around the world. In addition, farmers take pride in being good citizens in their community and in caring for their land and animals. There are approximately 70,000 hog farms in America today. Over the last 17 years, U.S. pork producers have dramatically decreased the need for antibiotics by lowering disease threats through sound herd management and by using drugs only when needed. U.S. pork producers take pride and personal responsibility in providing proper animal care on their farms. They consider anything short of providing the best, humane care possible as self-defeating. Today's consumer wants to purchase pork from pigs that have been raised under humane conditions. U.S pork producers know that good care and attention to the well-being and comfort of their animals is not only the right thing to do, it is an important responsibility they take seriously.

The modern farmer goes to great lengths to ensure his or her animals are raised in a clean, comfortable, disease-free environment. The pork industry is taking the lead in developing animal welfare standards that can be embraced by producers, packers, grocery stores, restaurants and consumers.

Poultry

In America's poultry industry today, family farmers work with production and processing companies to provide consumers with tasty, nutritious, and economical food. Poultry is the number-one protein purchased by American consumers, at more than 100 pounds per year for every man, woman and child. Clearly the poultry industry is selling what America wants.

America's poultry companies are responsible corporate citizens that work with thousands of farm families across the country and employ hundreds of thousands of people in safe, well-managed workplaces. The result is a very successful industry that produces, processes and markets the food products that Americans want and need. In poultry processing, interventions such as the use of chlorinated water in cleaning and chilling the birds are known to reduce the presence of microorganisms, including spoilage organisms. The practice of chilling poultry carcasses in ice-cold water is one of the most important decontamination steps in the process. Water chilling reduces bacterial contamination significantly. USDA records show that only about one chicken out of ten has any detectable level of

Salmonella on it, and usually the level is very low. Salmonella, like all such microorganisms, is destroyed by the heat of normal cooking.

Eggs

Egg farmers are committed to producing the safe, nutritious eggs, and the likelihood of getting a food borne illness from eggs is very low. When you handle eggs with care, they pose no greater food-safety risk than any other perishable food. You can ensure that your eggs will maintain their high quality and safety by using good hygiene, cooking, refrigeration and handling practices.

If bacteria are allowed to grow in or on food without being killed (usually by heat) before eating, food borne illness can result. However, in the rare event that an egg contains bacteria, you can reduce the risk by proper chilling and eliminate it by proper cooking.

The way food is processed and prepared is important because all foods have the ability to carry microorganisms (like bacteria and viruses) that can cause illness.

Along with other food and food-related organizations as well as government food and education agencies, egg farmers are members of the Partnership for Food Safety Education. This unique industry and government coalition has the aim of informing consumers about safe food-handling practices through the Fight BAC campaign.

Fish

Most US chef's work with local reputable seafood purveyors to obtain only the freshest seafood from local waters and beyond. They offer guests dozens of seafood varieties at the peak of their seasons, including Alaskan Halibut, Northwest Salmon, Hawaiian Mahi Mahi, Oregon Petrale Sole, Shrimp, Lobster, Crab, Clams and a large selection of oysters from the around the U.S just to name a few.

Culture Restaurants

You will experience restaurants in every type and class, from lavish expense-account *haute* and *nouvelle cuisine*. Italian, French, German, Indian, Chinese, Dutch, Thai, Greek, Mexican, Japanese sushi bars, Jewish, Korean, Russian, Hungarian, Polish and English pub grub. The most expensive restaurants will have that many staff, that they will outnumber the customers, the food will be excellent. It is difficult to generalize about American restaurants, the quality and price will vary greatly.

Because America is a new country and made up of immigrants, it is not known for any particular food other than Burgers, Peanut butter and Coke. However the immigrants brought with them knowledge and now produce the best of the food that their home country produced.

Italian immigrants brought with them the best of Italian food, Pasta, Spaghetti and Pizza; The Irish gave the US Guinness. The English introduced the best of English food; they left behind the worst, Tripe, Liver, Dripping, Mushy Peas and Sprouts. The Mexicans introduced tacos, the German's introduced Sausages. The advantage is you have the best food in the world in one place.

Waiters and waitresses are paid below minimum wage, typically $2-4 an hour. They make up there wage on tips. Please remember this and it's typically 20% of the bill. If you are from Europe or Australia you are used to tipping, here it is a must. Pardon the pun but let me give you a tip. Stick a

$20 bill on your table, next to your plate when ordering. I don't see the point of tipping after the meal, it's too late for them to give you and your guest's special service, but by showing you are going to give a decent tip at front, means you will be looked after. Many American waitresses will try to avoid the English and Australian's as they tip very little, one can hardly blame them.

Diners

You have seen them on the TV or in a film. They don't offer *nouvelle cuisine* but if you are looking for a quick non-fast food meal. Soups, and sandwiches are the norm, they will offer cooked breakfast all day and of course burgers and fries.

Coffee bars

One of the biggest surprises of visitors to the United States is the amount of coffee bars. Coffee bars are everywhere. In Manhattan NY there is one on almost every corner. For the average diner jockey, anything more than pocket change might seem like a lot to shell out for a cup of java. But if you learn how to use a coffee bar, you may find that it's the best deal in town. Most cafes have free newspapers, magazines, or books. Some even offer Internet connections so you can surf while you enjoy your cup of coffee. You don't have to buy a meal, and you don't have to keep refilling your beer mug. Coffee shops are made for hanging out. Bring your notebook, bring your sketch pad, and bring your PowerBooks. Forget about your college loans, your rent, and your boss. Sit back and watch the world go by after a couple cups of coffee, maybe you will be ready to get back on board. NEW YORK is not a hard place to find coffee: street vendors, delis and your own hotel room are among the prominent sources for the not very picky. And of course, there are plenty of cafes engineered to sell social scenes and designer sandwiches as much as coffee where you can kill a few hours. Apologies to the French, Spanish and Portuguese, but café their word for coffee has become associated as much with comfy chairs and the clickety-clack of laptops as with the beverage. But that's not what you need on your vacation. You need to get your quick caffeine fix in the most civilized way possible, and then be on your way.

Talk the Talk

The coffee bar world can be confusing if you don't understand coffee jargon. To help you out, we have compiled the following guide, with a bit of help from the menus of several dispensaries.

American, Drip or Regular Coffee - Your good-to-the-last-drop variety, but richer than anything you'll scoop from a can and fresher than what you're likely to get in most diners, restaurants or delis.

Barista - Coffee technician.

Bowls - Some places serve certain drinks, such as cafe au lait or hot chocolate, in a bowl. (Quote: "I can tell my mates that I went to America and had a bowl...of coffee" -- a cheeky Brit).

Cafe au Lait - A shot or two of espresso with steamed milk.

Caffe Americano - A shot of espresso diluted with hot water.

Caffeine - An addictive stimulant and diuretic derived from coffee, tea and kola nuts. A bitter white alkaloid.

Caffe Latte - A shot of espresso with steamed milk and lightly topped with foamed milk (note: much less foamed milk than a Cappuccino).

Caffe Mocha - A shot of espresso with chocolate syrup, steamed milk and topped with foamed milk or whipped cream.

Cappuccino - A shot of espresso with steamed and foamed milk (note: much more foam than a Caffe Latte).

Decaf - Most coffee bars offer decaffeinated coffee beverages; all the taste but minus the buzz.

Espresso - A concentrated coffee beverage produced with a method of brewing that uses pressure, rather than gravity, to pass hot water through a special blend and roast of ground coffee beans. Espresso is usually measured in "shots" of about 1 oz. to 1 1/2 oz.

Espresso Macchiato - A shot of espresso topped with foamed milk to keep it warm.

Espresso Con Panna - A shot of espresso topped with whipped cream.

Flavored Coffee Drinks - Hot and iced coffee drinks can be flavored with numerous syrups and liqueurs. Hard core coffee drinkers say these additives ruin their coffee. The usual lineup includes Amaretto, brandy, chocolate, chocolate almond, chocolate hazelnut, cinnamon, Drambuie, Grand Marnier, hazelnut, Irish Cream, Kalua (very nice with Cappuccino), rum, Sambuca, vanilla and whiskey.

Foamed Milk - Milk turned to foam by holding a steam nozzle just below the surface of a steel pitcher of milk (always steel so the Barista can feel the milk's temperature).

Foamed milk is used as insulation to keep espresso drinks warm.

High Test - A cup of coffee with caffeine in it (opposite of Unleaded Coffee -- see below)

Iced Coffee Drinks - Fresh-brewed coffee, cappuccino or espresso poured over ice. Beware of cafes that use yesterday's leftovers. For some reason iced coffee drinks are a little more expensive than hot ones. Ice costs, I guess, Starbucks call these frappuccino® beverages

Java - slang term for coffee; also a computer programming language.

Joe - another term for coffee.

Lungo - Espresso that has been "run long," meaning that more water is passed through the grinds. A Lungo is a bit milder than a regular espresso and comes in a slightly larger portion.

Ristretto - A "short run" of espresso, meaning a smaller, slightly stronger shot.

Schizo Coffee - A cup of coffee which includes equal parts of decaffeinated and regular coffee. Typically consumed by people trying to cut down their caffeine intake.

Steamed Milk - Milk heated to about 160 degrees by a jet of steam.

Unleaded Coffee - Synonym for decaffeinated coffee

Youth and Coffee bars.

If you come from most western countries around the world, you expect to see 16-20 yr olds, going to bars and night clubs. Often at closing time the local police will be in force due to drunken rowdy behavior, as the youth's walk home stopping in at take away restaurants to fill their hungry appetites. If you are a parent, Move to America and it will stop. In most states they can't and don't drink until they are 21.

The youth of United States will meet up at Diners or coffee bars. Starbucks is a favorite among them. They buy a variety of coffees and sit and talk, it becomes a meeting place, often live music is played and some snack food served. Over the past few years Christian music has grown from being found only in the church to other venues. Christian coffee houses have popped up as part of youth programs, outreach programs and even as standalone businesses. Live music can be found in a family atmosphere where no alcohol or smoking is allowed. Many coffee houses offer bible study and/or prayer time after the show. Local talent, regional talent and even some nationally recognized bands and artists perform at these shows and open mic nights allow newcomers to be heard. Not all are Christian; many such as Starbucks are with profit companies.

Fast Food

The modern history of fast-food in the United States of America began on 7 July 1912 with the opening of a fast food restaurant called the Automat, a cafeteria with its prepared foods behind small glass windows and coin-operated slots, in New York City, it created a sensation. Numerous Automat restaurants were quickly built around the country to deal with the demand. Automats remained extremely popular throughout the 1920s and 1930s. The company also popularized the notion of "take-out" food, with their slogan "Less work for Mother". The American company White Castle is generally credited with opening the second fast-food outlet in Wichita, Kansas in 1921, selling hamburgers for five cents apiece. Among its innovations, the company allowed customers to see the food being prepared. White Castle later added five holes to each beef patty to increase its surface area and speed cooking times. White Castle was successful from its inception and spawned numerous competitors.

McDonald's, the largest fast-food chain in the world and the brand most associated with the term "fast food," was founded as a barbecue drive-in in 1940 by Dick and Mac McDonald. After discovering that most of their profits came from hamburgers, the brothers closed their restaurant for three months and reopened it in 1948 as a walk-up stand offering a simple menu of hamburgers, French fries, shakes, coffee, and Coca-Cola, served in disposable paper wrapping. As a result, they were able to produce hamburgers and fries constantly, without waiting for customer orders, and could serve them immediately; hamburgers cost 15 cents, about half the price at a typical diner. Their streamlined production method, which they named the "Speedee Service System", was influenced by the production line innovations of Henry Ford. The McDonalds' stand was the milkshake machine company's biggest customer and a milkshake salesman named Ray Kroc traveled to California to discover the secret to their high-volume burger-and-shake operation. Kroc thought he could expand their concept, eventually buying the McDonalds' operation outright in 1961 with the goal of making cheap, ready-to-go hamburgers, French fries and milkshakes a nationwide business.

Kroc was the mastermind behind the rise of McDonald's as a national chain. The first part of his plan was to promote cleanliness in his restaurants. Kroc often took part at his own Des Plaines, Illinois, outlet by hosing down the garbage cans and scraping gum off the cement. Kroc also added great swaths of glass which enabled the customer to view the food preparation. This was very important to the American public which became quite germ conscious. A clean atmosphere was only part of Kroc's grander plan which separated McDonald's from the rest of the competition and attributes to their great success. Kroc envisioned making his restaurants appeal to families of suburbs. McDonald's restaurants are found in 120 countries and territories around the world and serve nearly 54 million customers each day.

Circa 2008

Modern commercial fast food is often highly processed and prepared in an industrial fashion, i.e., on a large scale with standard ingredients and standardized cooking and production methods. It is usually rapidly served in cartons or bags or in a plastic wrapping, in a fashion which minimizes cost. In most fast food operations, menu items are generally made from processed ingredients prepared at a central supply facility and then shipped to individual outlets where they are reheated, cooked (usually by microwave or deep-frying) or assembled in a short amount of time. This process ensures a consistent level of product quality, and is key to being able to deliver the order quickly to the customer and eliminate labor and equipment costs in the individual stores.

Because of commercial emphasis on speed, uniformity and low cost, fast food products are often made with ingredients formulated to achieve a certain flavor or consistency and to preserve freshness. Hydrogenated vegetable oils are pumped into fast foods which contain high amounts of Tran's fat. This requires a high degree of food engineering, the use of additives and processing techniques substantially alter the food from its original form and reduce its nutritional value. People in the United States spent $210 Billion in fast food restaurants in 2007.

Section 32) Taxation and the IRS.

It does not matter what country you come from all tax systems are complicated. The United States is no exception. You have to pay more than one form of income tax, although some states such as Florida you do not have to pay income tax. (But there are other taxes) If you are not going to live permanently in the United States and you are only going to own a holiday home, you will have very limited contact the IRS. If you are going to live in America, I would suggest an accountant. If you are buying a business, only a fool would try to complete their own tax returns. You will need a Certified Public Accountant, (CPA). To become a CPA, an accountant must take and pass a series of rigorous tests administered by the American Institute of Certified Public Accountants. A number of states also require CPAs to pass state exams as well. Accordingly, there are a number of accountants who never pass the CPA exam and though they can perform a variety of accountancy chores, they are not allowed to perform certain tasks that only a CPA can do. When many people hear or read the term accountant, the acronym CPA immediately comes to mind. Although these two expressions are related and may even be identical in meaning in some cases, there are differences between them. Get yourself a CPA. US federal income tax is levied on the world-wide income of US citizens and resident foreigners, and on certain types of US income of non-resident foreigners. If you earn an income in America, you need to file a US tax return; this still applies even if you are visiting the country.

Your Situation when you live in two countries and in particular, when you are moving permanently from one country to another. This involves the consideration of the tax systems in both countries with a view to minimizing your tax obligations in both.

The first thing you should do is talk to a CPA, and then you have to determine how you will treat by the tax authorities in each country. Are a going to be a resident or non-resident? This concept of tax residence causes a great deal of confusion. Tax residence can have different meanings in different countries. In the United States residence for tax purposes is not necessarily the same as residence for immigration purposes, you will be a resident for tax purposes, but you may also qualify as a resident for tax purposes even though you are not a resident for immigration purposes. This means you can be classified as a tax resident, even when you don't have a tourist visa. You can be a Non-Resident Alien, A resident Alien, An Illegal Alien, A Temporary Resident Alien, A Resident. You need to get this correct. If you are an alien (not a U.S. citizen), you are considered a nonresident alien unless you meet one of two tests. You are a resident alien of the United States for tax purposes if you meet either the green card test or the substantial presence test for the calendar year (January 1-December 31).

Certain rules exist for determining the Residency Beginning and Ending Dates for aliens. In some cases aliens are allowed to make elections which override the green card test and the substantial presence test.

Taxation of Nonresident Aliens

How Income Is Categorized and Taxed? A nonresident alien's income that is subject to U.S. income tax must be divided into two categories:

Income that is effectively connected with a trade or business in the United States

Income that is not effectively connected with a trade or business in the United States

What is the Difference Between Effectively Connected and Not Effectively Connected Income?

The difference between these two categories is that Effectively Connected Income, after allowable deductions, is taxed at graduated rates. These are the same rates that apply to U.S. citizens and residents. Income that is not effectively connected is taxed at a flat 30% (or lower treaty rate) and no deductions are allowed against such income. Income that is not effectively connected is also known as Fixed, Determinable, Annual, or Periodical (FDAP). Nonresident aliens who are required to file an income tax return should use Form 1040NR or, if qualified, Form 1040NR-EZ. Refer to the Instructions for Form 1040NR-EZ to determine if you may use Form 1040NR-EZ. If you do not qualify to file Form 1040NR-EZ, you must file Form 1040NR. *Confused? See a CPA.*

Taxation of Resident Aliens

A resident alien's income is generally subject to tax in the same manner as a U.S. citizen. If you are a resident alien, you must report all interest, dividends, wages, or other compensation for services, income from rental property or royalties, and other types of income on your U.S. tax return. You must report these amounts whether from sources within or outside the United States. Resident aliens are generally taxed in the same way as U.S. citizens. This means that their worldwide income is subject to U.S. tax and must be reported on their U.S. tax return. Income of resident aliens is subject to the graduated tax rates that apply to U.S. citizens. Resident aliens use the Tax Table and Tax Rate

Schedules which apply to U.S. citizens found in the instructions for Forms 1040, 1040A, or 1040EZ.

Resident aliens can use the same filing statuses available to U.S. citizens. You can claim the same deductions allowed to U.S. citizens if you are a resident alien for the entire tax year. You should get Form 1040 and its instructions for more information on how to claim your allowable deductions. You can claim personal exemptions and exemptions for dependents according to the dependency rules for U.S. citizens. You can claim an exemption for your spouse on a Married Filing Separate return if your spouse had no gross income for U.S. tax purposes and was not the dependent of another taxpayer. You can claim this exemption even if your spouse has not been a resident alien for a full tax year or is an alien who has not come to the United States. You can claim an exemption for each person who qualifies as a dependent according to the rules for U.S. citizens. The dependent must be a citizen or national of the United States or be a resident of the United States, Canada, or Mexico for some part of the calendar year in which your tax year begins. Your spouse and each dependent must have either a Social Security Number or an Individual Tax Identification Number in order to be claimed as an exemption or a dependent. Resident aliens should file Form 1040EZ, Income Tax Return for Single and Joint Filers with No Dependents, Form 1040A, U.S. Individual Income Tax Return or Form 1040, U.S. Individual Income Tax Return at the address shown in the instructions for those forms. The due date for filing the return and paying any tax due is April 15 of the year following the year for which you are filing a return. You are allowed an automatic extension to June 15 to file if your main place of business and the home you live in are outside the United States and Puerto Rico on April 15. You can get an automatic extension of time to file until October15 by filing Form 4868 on or before April 15 (June 15 if you qualify for the June 15 extension). *Confused? See a CPA.*

Dual Status Aliens

Dual status aliens determine their residency status under both the Internal Revenue Code and tax treaties. If you change status during the current year-from a nonresident alien to a resident alien Or from a resident alien to a nonresident alien. Aliens who make such a change are Dual Status Aliens and must file a special tax return called a Dual Status Return described in Publication 519. If you are a Nonresident Alien who will become a Resident Alien under the Substantial Presence test in the year following this taxable year, you may elect to be treated as a Dual Status Alien for this taxable year and a Resident Alien for the next taxable year if you meet certain tests. (Refer to section "Dual-Status Aliens" – "First Year Choice" in Publication 519, U.S. Tax Guide for Aliens.) A dual status alien married to a U.S. citizen or to a resident alien may elect to file a joint income tax return with his/her U.S. citizen or resident alien spouse. Refer to "Nonresident Spouse Treated as a Resident" in Publication 519, U.S. Tax Guide for Aliens. *Confused? See a CPA.*

The most basic decisions you will have to make when planning your tax affairs are whether to cease to be a resident in your home country, whether to cease to be ordinary resident in that country and whether to change your domicile to the United States. Each of these has many consequences, many of which are not obvious. Another consideration is when in the tax year to make these changes. If you get this wrong it could cost you thousands in unnecessary tax payments, not to mention the stress, inconvenience and frustration. I can't stress enough how important this is, Please seek help from a CPA and an accountant in your home country.

Sales Tax

A sales tax is a consumption tax charged at the point of purchase for certain goods and services. The tax is usually set as a percentage by the government charging the tax. There is usually a list of exemptions. The tax can be included in the price (tax-inclusive) or added at the point of sale (tax-exclusive).

Ideally, a sales tax is fair, has a high compliance rate, is difficult to avoid, is charged exactly once on any one item, and is simple to calculate and simple to collect. A conventional or retail sales tax attempts to achieve this by charging the tax only on the final end user, unlike a gross receipts tax levied on the intermediate business that purchases materials for production or ordinary operating expenses prior to delivering a service or product to the marketplace. This prevents so-called tax "cascading" or "pyramiding," in which an item is taxed more than once as it makes its way from production to final retail sale. There are several types of sales taxes: Seller or Vendor Taxes, Consumer Excise Taxes, Retail Transaction Taxes, or Value Added Taxes.

Not only does each State have different Sales Tax rates, but each county in that state may have different sales tax rates. Typically they are 5-7.5%

State	Tax Rates	Food	Prescription Drugs	Non-prescription Drugs
ALABAMA	4		*	
ALASKA	none			
ARIZONA	5.6	*	*	
ARKANSAS	6		*	
CALIFORNIA (3)	7.25 (2)	*	*	
COLORADO	2.9	*	*	
CONNECTICUT	6	*	*	*
DELAWARE	none			
FLORIDA	6	*	*	*
GEORGIA	4	* (4)	*	
HAWAII	4		*	
IDAHO	6		*	
ILLINOIS (2)	6.25	1%	1%	1%
INDIANA	6	*	*	
IOWA	5	*	*	
KANSAS	5.3		*	
KENTUCKY	6	*	*	
LOUISIANA	4	* (4)	*	
MAINE	5	*	*	
MARYLAND	5	*	*	*
MASSACHUSETTS	5	*	*	
MICHIGAN	6	*	*	
MINNESOTA	6.5	*	*	*
MISSISSIPPI	7		*	
MISSOURI	4.225	1.225	*	
MONTANA	none			
NEBRASKA	5.5	*	*	
NEVADA	6.5	*	*	
NEW HAMPSHIRE	none			
NEW JERSEY	7	*	*	*

NEW MEXICO	5	*	*
NEW YORK	4	*	*	*
NORTH CAROLINA (5)	4.25	* (4)	*
NORTH DAKOTA	5	*	*
OHIO	5.5	*	*
OKLAHOMA	4.5		*
OREGON	none		
PENNSYLVANIA	6	*	*	*
RHODE ISLAND	7	*	*	*
SOUTH CAROLINA (6)	5	3%	*
SOUTH DAKOTA	4		*
TENNESSEE	7	6%	*
TEXAS	6.25	*	*	*
UTAH	4.75	2.75%	*
VERMONT	6	*	*	*
VIRGINIA	5 (2)	2.5% (2)	*	*
WASHINGTON	6.5	*	*
WEST VIRGINIA	6	5%	*
WISCONSIN	5	*	*
WYOMING	4	* (7)	*
DIST. OF COLUMBIA	5.75	*	*	*

The table shows each State flat Sales tax rate, this is added to item when you buy them. If you pick something up in a store for $2.00, when you go to pay you will have tax added. Plus the local county rate, for example in Florida Manatee County you will have to pay 6.5%. If you cross over the road (University Parkway) to Sarasota County you will have to pay 7%. Why? The additional .5% the local voters voted for

248

it! The tax is expected to bring in about $1.4 billion over 15 years. It will maintain the sales tax in Sarasota County at 7 percent. If the renewal had failed, the tax in 2009 would have decreased to 6 %. Since it went into effect in 1989, the 1 percent tax has paid for $760 million into government projects, including widening roads, school renovations. Half the revenue raised by the tax will go to Sarasota County government, one-quarter to county schools and the rest divided among the cities of Sarasota, Venice and North Port and the town of Longboat Key. The Good people of Sarasota wish to keep their city the best in America, in the last 10 years Siesta Key beach in Sarasota has been voted the best beach in the world a record 7 times. In 2002 it was voted the best city in the world to live, I guess they wish to keep it this way.

Section 33) Telephone and Cell Phones Providers.

Like all western countries, America is driven on technology. The cell phone industry in the United States is huge, Even Richard Branson has launched Virgin phones, although 6 years on and it's not very popular. Traditional phone companies Bell, AT&T and Verizon where front runners, but have lost ground to MetroPcs.

If you need a cell phone, go to MetroPcs they will offer a phone without a contract, completely unlimited calling, text and International text for $45 per month! No company can come close. You can add money to the account this is called Metro-Connect and can call around the world for 2-3 cents per minute. The company is the fastest growing cell company in the United States. Its' not hard to see why.

Home phones are expensive, you would typically pay $50 a month and have to pay extra for long distance, many home owners have now cancelled the home phones and changed to MetroPcs and use this as the home phone. If you do want a traditional phone, you will get a lot of telesales calls up to 9pm 7 days a week. Internet services are carried by cable, so you do not need a phone line, (Land line)

Section 34) Climate Across the States.

Due to its size, the United States has just about every range you can expect anywhere in the world. From the North of Alaska to the Swamps and tropical Florida Everglades, Lush green of Kentucky to the Nevada desert. The United States climate varies enormously, plus if you come from Europe it will surprise you to discover the rapid changes. New York can get over 90 in the summer, and always gets down to freezing snow in the winter.

Florida FL:

You can almost always tip your hat to the end of another perfect day in Florida. The climate has always been Florida's most important natural resources, which is reflected in its official nickname, the "Sunshine State." You will wake up every day to a Blue sky.

Summers throughout the state are long, warm, and fairly humid. Winters are mild with periodic invasions of cool to occasionally cold air. Coastal areas in all sections of Florida average slightly warmer temperatures in winter and cooler ones in summer.

The primary factors affecting the state's climate are latitude and numerous inland lakes. Proximity to the currents of the Atlantic Ocean and the Gulf of Mexico also plays an important role. Florida gets most of its rain during the hot summer when it is needed, the rain will last approx 15-30 minutes. Within 15 after the rain, the sun will be shinning and the temperature back up to the 90's.

Key West: Key West's coldest month is January when the average temperature overnight is 65.2°F. In August, the

251

warmest month, the average day time temperature rises to 89.5°F. The driest month in Key West is February with 1.51 inches of precipitation, and with 5.45 inches September is the wettest month.

Sarasota: Sarasota's coldest month is January when the average temperature overnight is 59.4°F. In August, the warmest month, the average day time temperature rises to 90.4°F. The driest month in Sarasota is November with 1.62 inches of precipitation, and with 7.86 inches August is the wettest month. July and August is known in Sarasota as the rainy season. The rain will fall normally in the afternoon for approx 20-30 minutes. 10 minutes later the sun is back out and the temperature back up to 90+.

Pensacola: Pensacola's coldest month is January when the average temperature overnight is 43.7°F. In July, the warmest month, the average day time temperature rises to 90.7°F. The driest month in Pensacola is April with 3.89 inches of precipitation, and with 8.02 inches July is the wettest month.

California CA:

In general, summers are hot, winters are mild and humidity is low. Offshore breezes keep the beach communities of Los Angeles and San Diego cooler in summer and warmer in winter than those further inland. Temperatures in the summer can get well over 90°F (32°C) and smog can become a problem. In winter temperatures get down to around 55°F (12°C) and rain is a possibility. San Francisco, a little further north, is a little cooler and breezier and there is regularly fog over the harbor until about midday. Generally the weather is warm and dry in all seasons, with 354 days of sunshine a year. Westerly winds from the ocean also bring moisture, and the northern parts of the state generally receive higher annual rainfall amounts than the south. California's mountain ranges influence the climate as well: moisture-laden air from the west cools as it ascends the mountains, dropping moisture; some of the rainiest parts of the state are west-facing mountain slopes. Northwestern California has a temperate climate with rainfall of 15–50 inches (400–1,270 mm) per year. Some areas of Coast Redwood forest receive over 100 inches of precipitation per year (2,540 mm).

California Santa Ana winds. Santa Anas are hot, high winds that blow from the eastern mountains and deserts towards coastal Southern California, usually in the spring and fall. They are the result of air pressure buildup between the Sierra Nevada and the Rocky Mountains. This air mass spills out, is pulled by gravity, and circulates clockwise around the high pressure area, bringing winds from the east and northeast; as the air descends in elevation, it heats up and the humidity plummets to less than 15%. It is often said that the air is heated and dried as it passes through the nearby deserts, but according to meteorologists this is a popular misconception; during Santa Ana conditions, it is typically hotter along the coast than in the deserts. As the Santa Ana winds are channeled through the mountain passes they can approach hurricane force.

Nevada NV:

Ely: Ely's coldest month is January when the average temperature overnight is 10.4°F. In July, the warmest month, the average day time temperature rises to 87.3°F. The driest month in Ely is December with 0.50 inches of precipitation, and with 1.29 inches May is the wettest month.

Las Vegas: Las Vegas's coldest month is December when the average temperature overnight is 36.6°F. In July, the warmest month, the average day time temperature rises to 104.1°F. The driest month in Las Vegas is June with 0.08 inches of precipitation, and with 0.69 inches February is the wettest month. Las Vegas (often abbreviated as "Vegas") is the most populous city in the state of Nevada, United States, the seat of Clark County, and an internationally renowned resort, shopping, entertainment, and gambling destination. It was established in 1905 and officially became a city in 1911. With the growth that followed, Las Vegas became the largest U.S. city founded in the 20th century (a distinction held by Chicago in the 19th century). It is the 28th largest city in the United States. Las Vegas started as a stopover on the pioneer trails to the west and became a popular railroad town in the early 1900s. It was a staging point for all the mines in the surrounding area, especially those around the town of Bullfrog, that shipped their goods out to the rest of the country. With the growth of the railroads, Las Vegas became less important, but the completion of the nearby Hoover Dam resulted in substantial growth in tourism, which, along with the legalization of gambling, led to the advent of the casino-hotels for which Las Vegas is famous.

Reno: Reno's coldest month is December when the average temperature overnight is 20.7°F. In July, the warmest month, the average day time temperature rises to 91.2°F. The driest month in Reno is July with 0.24 inches of precipitation, and with 1.06 inches January is the wettest month.

Arizona AZ:

Arizona is the sixth largest state in area, after New Mexico and before Nevada. Of the state's 118,000 square miles (306,000 km²), approximately 15% is privately owned. The remaining area is government forest and park land, recreation areas and Native American reservations.

Arizona is best known for its desert landscape, which is rich in plants such as cactus. It is also known for its climate, which presents exceptionally hot summers and mild winters. Less well known is the pine-covered high country of the Colorado Plateau in the north-central portion of the state.

Like other states of the Southwest, Arizona has an abundance of topographical characteristics in addition to its desert climate. More than half of the state features mountains and plateaus and contains the largest stand of Ponderosa pine in the United States. The Mogollon Rim, a 2000-foot (600 m) escarpment, cuts across the central section of the state and marks the southwestern edge of the Colorado Plateau, where the state experienced its worst forest fire ever in 2002. Arizona belongs firmly within the Basin and Range region of North America. The region was shaped by prehistoric volcanism, followed by a cooling-off and related subsidence. The entire region is slowly sinking.

The Grand Canyon is a colorful, steep-sided gorge, carved by the Colorado River, in northern Arizona. The canyon is one of the seven natural wonders of the world and is largely contained in the Grand Canyon National Park—one of the first national parks in the United States. President Theodore Roosevelt was a major proponent of designating the Grand Canyon area, visiting on numerous occasions to hunt mountain lion and enjoy the scenery.

New York State NY:

The climate of New York State is broadly representative of the humid continental type, which prevails in the northeastern United States, but its diversity is not usually encountered within an area of comparable size. The geographical position of the state and the usual course of air masses, governed by the large-scale patterns of atmospheric circulation, provide general climatic controls. Differences in latitude, character of the topography, and proximity to large bodies of water have pronounced effects on the climate.

Nearly all storm and frontal systems moving eastward across the continent pass through or in close proximity to **New York State.** Storm systems often move northward along **the Atlantic coast** and have an important influence on the weather and climate of Long Island and the lower Hudson Valley. Frequently, areas deep in the interior of the state feel the effects of such coastal storms.

Cold winter temperatures prevail over New York whenever Arctic air masses, under high barometric pressure, flow southward from central Canada or from Hudson Bay. High-pressure systems often move just off the Atlantic coast, become more or less stagnant for several days, and then a persistent airflow from the southwest or south affects the state. This circulation brings the very warm, often humid weather of the summer season and the mild, more pleasant temperatures during the fall, winter, and spring seasons. During April and May and again in October and November you can rely on a sweater, sport jacket, light raincoat or parka. By November bring along a scarf and gloves. December through early March count on temperatures near or below freezing at least for part of the day, plus the possibility of real snow storms, freezing rain and bitter cold winds, especially in January. But the weather here is variable and some years there is no snow. Waterproof foot wear is highly recommended. June, July, especially August and even early September can be very hot and humid with amazing thunderstorms which pass quickly. In August and September, New York, often gets tropical storms and occasionally a hurricane. Bring light summer clothing plus a light sweater to avoid freezing in the many air conditioned buildings including museums and office buildings.

North Carolina NC:

While North Carolina is located in a warm temperate zone, its diverse regions can experience a great variety of weather conditions. While locations in the mountains may see average temperatures of 30 degrees Fahrenheit in January and 65 degrees Fahrenheit in August, locations in the coastal plains can often experience January averages in the mid 40's and August averages in the 90's. The state averages 44 inches of rainfall each year, and 5 inches of snow. Western North Carolina's majestic landscape features the Blue Ridge Mountains and the Great Smoky Mountains, which help make up the Appalachian Mountains, possibly the oldest mountain range in the United States. The region is also home to Mount Mitchell. Rising 6,684 feet above sea level, Mount Mitchell is the tallest peak east of the Mississippi River. The Eastern Continental Divide runs along the top of the Blue Ridge Mountains, separating the rivers flowing east from those flowing west. Rivers that fall on the eastern side of the divide flow toward the Atlantic Ocean while those on the western side of the divide flow toward the Tennessee and Ohio rivers and into the Gulf of Mexico.

South Carolina SC:

South Carolina has a humid, subtropical climate. Average temperatures range from 68°F (20°C) on the coast to 58°F (14°C) in the northwest, with colder temperatures in the mountains. Summers are hot: in the central part of the state, temperatures often exceed 90°F (32°C), with a record of 111°F (44°C) set at Camden on 28 June 1954. In the northwest, temperatures of 32°F(0°C) or less occur from 50 to 70 days a year; the record low for the state is −20°F (−29°C), set at Caesars Head Mountain on 18 January 1977. The daily mean temperature at Columbia is 44°F(7°C) in January and 81°F (27°C) in July.

Rainfall is ample throughout the state, averaging 48.3 in (122.7 cm) annually at Columbia (1971–2000) and ranging from 38 in (97 cm) in the central region to 52 in (132 cm) in the upper piedmont. Snow and sleet (averaging 2 in/5 cm a year at Columbia) occur about three times annually, but more frequently and heavily in the mountains. South Carolina mammals include white-tailed deer (the state animal), black bear, opossum, gray and red foxes, cottontail and marsh rabbits, mink, and woodchuck. Three varieties of raccoon are indigenous, one of them unique to Hilton Head Island. The state is also home to Bachman's shrew, originally identified in South Carolina by John Bachman, one of John J. Audubon's collaborators. Common birds include the mockingbird and Carolina wren (the state bird). Twenty-two animal species were listed as threatened or endangered in South Carolina in 2003, including the Indiana bat, Carolina heelsplitter, bald eagle, five species of sea turtle, wood stork, and shortnose sturgeon.

Washington WA:

The climate in Washington varies across the state from east to west, and the state is divided both geographically and climatically by the Cascade Mountain range. The western part of Washington tends to be mild and humid, and is one of the world's rainiest areas, while the eastern region is cooler and drier with a more continental type of climate, experiencing hot summers and cold winters. Western

Washington often experiences heavy cloud cover, fog and drizzle, and although summers tend to be sunny, they are milder than in the east. In the western area, average temperatures in summer can range from 44°F (7°C) on the slope of the Western Cascade Mountains (which experience some of the heaviest snowfall in the US) to 80°F (27°C) in the foothills, while winter temperatures range from 20°F (-7°C) on the western slopes of the Cascades to 48°F (9°C) along the Pacific coast. The average temperatures in Eastern Washington are more extreme, with summer temperatures ranging from a cool 48°F (9°C) on slope of the Eastern Cascades to 92°F (33°C) in the south-central part of the state and winter temperatures range from 8°F (-13°C) in the northeastern Cascades to 40°F (4°C) on the southeastern plateau. Rainfall in Seattle is usually heaviest from October to March.

Texas TX:

Texas's climate varies widely, from arid in the west to wet in the east. Due to its large size, (Texas is by far the largest State) Texas is home to several different climates. Texas ranks first in tornado occurrence with an average of 139 per year. There are several distinct climate regions the names of which are not official: Northern Plains, Big Bend Country, Texas Hill Country, Piney Woods, and South Texas.

The Northern Plains's climate can best be described as Humid but it is prone to drought due to climate change. Annually it receives anywhere between 16 to 32 inches of rain. Tornadoes, caused by the convergence of northern and southern prevailing winds are not uncommon, making the region part of the tornado alley. Poor land management, drought, and high wind speeds can cause large dust storms, kept to minimum in modern times, but most troublesome in the 1930s during the great depression. The panhandle region, unprotected by the warm gulf currents experiences colder winters than the other regions of Texas.

The Big Bend Country is the farthest west region in geography. It is also the driest receiving an average annual rainfall of only 16 inches or less. The arid climate is the main reason for desertification of the land, but overgrazing is slowly widening the land area of that desert. In the mountain areas one can see coniferous forests in a wetter and more temperate environment. Winds are strengthened as they are forced to push through canyons and valleys. In the flatter areas these winds are harvested into usable electricity.

The Texas Hill Country, or central Texas is shaped by its many rivers and hills. The climate is Subtropical, with cool winters and hot summers. The vegetation is both deciduous in the river valleys, and coniferous where there is greater elevation. In a single year the region can receive up to 48 inches of rain, and flooding is common near rivers and in low lying areas. The Piney Woods is the eastern region of Texas. It receives the most rainfall; more than 48 inches annually in the far east. This is due to the gulf currents that carry humid air to the region, where it condenses and precipitates. Hurricanes also strike the region, the most disastrous of which was the Galveston Hurricane of 1900. More recently hurricanes Rita and Katrina pummeled the coastline. The humidity of the region greatly amplifies the feeling of heat during the summer. The winters are kept moderate by warm gulf currents. The region of South Texas includes the semiarid ranch country and the wetter Rio Grande Valley. Considered to be the southernmost tip of the American Great Plains region, its rainfall is similar to that of the Northern Plains. The coastal areas are nearly warm year round. Subtropical forests line the Rio Grande River. Inland, where it is drier, ranches dominate the landscape, characterized by thick spiny brush. The winters are very mild and dry, and the summers hot and humid.

Michigan MI

Alpena: Alpena's coldest month is January when the average temperature overnight is 9.5°F. In July, the warmest month, the average day time temperature rises to 79.0°F. The driest month in Alpena is February with 1.35 inches of precipitation, and with 3.50 inches August is the wettest month.

Detroit: Detroit's coldest month is January when the average temperature overnight is 17.8°F. In July, the warmest month, the average day time temperature rises to 83.4°F. The driest month in Detroit is February with 1.88 inches of precipitation, and with 3.55 inches June is the wettest month.

Grand Rapids: Grand Rapids' coldest month is January when the average temperature overnight is 15.6°F. In July, the warmest month, the average day time temperature rises to 82.3°F. The driest month in Grand Rapids is February with 1.53 inches of precipitation, and with 4.28 inches September is the wettest month.

Lansing: Lansing's coldest month is January when the average temperature overnight is 13.9°F. In July, the warmest month, the average day time temperature rises to 82.1°F. The driest month in Lansing is February with 1.45 inches of precipitation, and with 3.60 inches June is the wettest month.

Marguette: Marquette's coldest month is January when the average temperature overnight is 3.3°F. In July, the warmest month, the average day time temperature rises to 75.2°F.

The driest month in Marquette is February with 1.85 inches of precipitation, and with 3.74 inches September is the wettest month.

Sault Ste, Marie: Sault Ste. Marie's coldest month is January when the average temperature overnight is 4.9°F. In July, the warmest month, the average day time temperature rises to 75.7°F. The driest month in Sault Ste. Marie is February with 1.60 inches of precipitation, and with 3.71 inches September is the wettest month.

Montana MT:

Billings: Billings' coldest month is January when the average temperature overnight is 15.1°F. In July, the warmest month, the average day time temperature rises to 85.8°F. The driest month in Billings is February with 0.57 inches of precipitation, and with 2.48 inches May is the wettest month.

Great Falls: Great Fall's coldest month is January when the average temperature overnight is 11.3°F. In July, the warmest month, the average day time temperature rises to 82.0°F. The driest month in Great Falls is February with 0.51 inches of precipitation, and with 2.53 inches May is the wettest month.

Helena: Helena's coldest month is January when the average temperature overnight is 9.9°F. In July, the warmest month, the average day time temperature rises to 83.4°F. The driest month in Helena is February with 0.38 inches of precipitation, and with 1.82 inches June is the wettest month.

North Dakota ND:

Bismarck: Bismarck's coldest month is January when the average temperature overnight is -0.6°F. In July, the warmest month, the average day time temperature rises to 84.5°F. The driest month in Bismarck is December with 0.44 inches of precipitation, and with 2.59 inches June is the wettest month.

Fargo: Fargo's coldest month is January when the average temperature overnight is -2.3°F. In July, the warmest month, the average day time temperature rises to 82.2°F. The driest month in Fargo is December with 0.57 inches of precipitation, and with 3.51 inches June is the wettest month.

Williston: Williston's coldest month is January when the average temperature overnight is -3.3°F. In July, the warmest month, the average day time temperature rises to 83.4°F. The driest month in Williston is February with 0.39 inches of precipitation, and with 2.36 inches June is the wettest month.

South Dakota SD:

Huron: Huron's coldest month is January when the average temperature overnight is 3.5°F. In July, the warmest month, the average day time temperature rises to 86.1°F. The driest month in Huron is December with 0.39 inches of precipitation, and with 3.28 inches June is the wettest month.

Rapid City: Rapid City's coldest month is January when the average temperature overnight is 11.3°F. In July, the warmest month, the average day time temperature rises to 85.5°F. The driest month in Rapid City is January with 0.37

inches of precipitation, and with 2.96 inches May is the wettest month.

Alaska AK:

Anchorage: Anchorage's coldest month is January when the average temperature overnight is 9.3°F. In July, the warmest month, the average day time temperature rises to 65.3°F. The driest month in Anchorage is April with 0.52 inches of precipitation, and with 2.93 inches August is the wettest month.

Juneau: Juneau's coldest month is January when the average temperature overnight is 20.7°F. In July, the warmest month, the average day time temperature rises to 64.3°F. The driest month in Juneau is April with 2.96 inches of precipitation, and with 8.30 inches October is the wettest month.

Nome: Nome's coldest month is February when the average temperature overnight is -2.3°F. In July, the warmest month, the average day time temperature rises to 58.6°F. The driest month in Nome is March with 0.60 inches of precipitation, and with 3.23 inches August is the wettest month.

Ohio OH:

Cleveland: Cleveland's coldest month is January when the average temperature overnight is 18.8°F. In July, the warmest month, the average day time temperature rises to 81.4°F. The driest month in Cleveland is February with 2.29 inches of precipitation, and with 3.89 inches June is the wettest month.

Columbus: Columbus's coldest month is January when the average temperature overnight is 20.3°F. In July, the warmest month, the average day time temperature rises to 85.3°F. The driest month in Columbus is February with 2.20 inches of precipitation, and with 4.61 inches July is the wettest month.

Dayton: Dayton's coldest month is January when the average temperature overnight is 19.0°F. In July, the warmest month, the average day time temperature rises to 84.2°F. The driest month in Dayton is February with 2.29 inches of precipitation, and with 4.21 inches June is the wettest month.

Toledo: Toledo's coldest month is January when the average temperature overnight is 16.4°F. In July, the warmest month, the average day time temperature rises to 83.4°F. The driest month in Toledo is February with 1.88 inches of precipitation, and with 3.80 inches June is the wettest month.

Illinois IL:

Chicago: Known around the world as the 'windy city'. It's not actually due to the weather. Chicago's average wind speeds 10.4 mph (16.7 km/h) are no greater than several other major American cities. For example, Boston has an average wind speed of 12.5 mph (20.1 km/h), and tops the list for the windiest large US city while New York City's Kennedy Airport averages 12.2 mph (19.6 km/h). The name was actually given to the city over 100 years ago. The nickname Windy City fell on Chicago due to its behavior during the bidding for the 'World's Fair' of 1893. The bidding was fierce and New York was one of the rivals. *The New York Sun* editor Charles Dana wrote about Chicago's bid lobbying: "Don't pay attention to the nonsensical claims of that windy city. Its people could not build a world's fair even if they won it."Chicago's coldest month is January when the average temperature overnight is 14.3°F. In July, the warmest month, the average day time temperature rises to 83.5°F. The driest month in Chicago is February with 1.63 inches of precipitation, and with 4.62 inches August is the wettest month.

Springfield: Springfield's coldest month is January when the average temperature overnight is 17.1°F. In July, the warmest month, the average day time temperature rises to 86.5°F. The driest month in Springfield is January with 1.62 inches of precipitation, and with 4.06 inches May is the wettest month.

Tennessee TN:

Chattanooga: Chattanooga's coldest month is January when the average temperature overnight is 29.9°F. In July, the warmest month, the average day time temperature rises to 89.8°F. The driest month in Chattanooga is October with 3.26 inches of precipitation, and with 6.19 inches March is the wettest month.

Nashville: Nashville's coldest month is January when the average temperature overnight is 27.9°F. In July, the warmest month, the average day time temperature rises to 88.7°F. The driest month in Nashville is October with 2.87 inches of precipitation, and with 5.07 inches May is the wettest month.

Memphis: Memphis's coldest month is January when the average temperature overnight is 31.3°F. In July, the warmest month, the average day time temperature rises to 92.1°F. The driest month in Memphis is August with 3.00 inches of precipitation, and with 5.79 inches April is the wettest month.

Section 35) Pets: Taking the Smaller Members of Your Family.

The simple answer is yes. The import of animals and birds into America are no different to any other civilized western country. Therefore subject to health, quarantine, agriculture, wildlife and customs regulations. You can travel with your pet within continental United States; it is not unusual to see passengers carrying a small dog or cat on a plane flying from one part of the country to another. Pets, particularly dogs and cats must be examined at the first point of entry. If you are coming from a non rabies country such as the UK, you have 7 days to take your pet to a vet. If your pet is excluded from entry it must be returned to the original country or destroyed. Sadly, while awaiting disposition, pets will be detained at the owner's expense at the port of arrival.

Travelers frequently ask about taking their pets with them to the United States. All such importation is subject to health, quarantine, agriculture, wildlife, and customs requirements and prohibitions. Pets taken out of the United States and returned are subject to the same requirements as those entering for the first time.

The U.S. Public Health Service requires that pet dogs and cats brought into this country be examined at the first port of entry for evidence of diseases that can be transmitted to humans. Dogs coming from areas not free of rabies must be accompanied by a valid rabies vaccination certificate. Turtles are subject to certain restrictions, and monkeys may not be imported as pets under any circumstances.

Circa 2007

The U.S. Fish and Wildlife Service are concerned with the importation, trade, sale, and taking of wildlife and with protecting endangered plant and animal species. Some wildlife species of dogs, cats, turtles, reptiles, and birds, although imported as pets, may be listed as endangered. Endangered and threatened animal and plant wildlife, migratory birds, marine mammals, and certain injurious wildlife may not be imported without special federal permits. Sportsmen will find the section on wildlife of particular interest, since game birds and animals are subject to special entry requirements.

You should also check with state, county, and municipal authorities for local restrictions on importing pets.

All birds and animals must be imported under healthy, humane conditions. U.S. Department of Agriculture (USDA) regulations require that careful arrangements be made with the carrier for suitable cages, space, ventilation, and protection from the elements. Cleaning, feeding, watering, and other necessary services must be provided. Under the Animal Welfare Act, the Department of Agriculture is responsible for setting the standards concerning the transportation, handling, care, and treatment of animals.

Every imported container of pets, or package of animal parts or products, must be plainly marked, labeled or tagged on the outside with the names and addresses of the shipper and consignee, along with an accurate invoice specifying the number of each species contained in the shipment.

Since hours of service and availability of inspectors from the other agencies involved may vary from port to port, you are strongly urged to check with your anticipated port of arrival before importing a pet or other animal. This will assure expeditious processing and reduce the possibility of unnecessary delays. Dogs, cats, and turtles are free of duty. Other pets imported into the United States, if subject to a customs duty, may be included in your customs exemption if they accompany you and are imported for your personal use and not for sale.

Purebred animals other than domesticated livestock that are imported for breeding purposes are free of duty under certain conditions. A declaration is required to show that the importer is a citizen of the United States; that the animal is imported specifically for breeding purposes; that it is identical with the description in the certificate of pedigree presented; and that it is registered in the country of origin in a book of registry recognized by the U.S. Department of Agriculture. An application to the Department of Agriculture on VS Form 17-338 for a certificate of pure breeding must be furnished before the animal is examined at the designated port of entry. All birds -- those taken out of the country as well as those being returned -- are subject to controls and restrictions. In addition, nearly all birds coming into the country require a permit from the U.S. Fish and Wildlife Service. Birds must be quarantined upon arrival for at least 30 days in a USDA-operated facility at the owner's expense. These facilities are located at the following ports of entry:

New York, NY	McAllen, TX	Miami, FL
(718)553-1727	(210)782-7995	(305)526-2926

San Ysidro, CA	Los Angeles, CA
(310)215-2352	(310)215-1314

(California reservations should be made in Los Angeles.)

A 30-day quarantine costs approximately $200 per bird; cost is subject to change.

A health certificate executed by the national veterinarian of the country of export must accompany the bird. The certificate must have been executed no more than 30 days prior to the bird's arrival. This certificate must affirm that the bird has been examined, that it shows no evidence of communicable disease, and that it is being exported in accordance with the laws of that country. VS Form 17-23 may be used for this purpose.

The bird must be removed from the quarantine facility within five days of notification of release. It is the owner's responsibility to arrange for the bird's transportation and to pay the costs of quarantine.

Birds from Canada that have been in the owner's possession for at least 90 days before importation and that are found healthy upon veterinary inspection at one of the Canadian border ports of entry where veterinarians are stationed are exempt from the 30-day quarantine.

Pet birds originating in the United States may be re-imported without being quarantined if they are accompanied by a United States veterinary health certificate and, if necessary, a permit from the U.S. Fish and Wildlife Service. This health certificate must be obtained prior to departure from the United States and must include a leg band or tattoo number.

Pet birds must be kept separate and apart from all other birds and poultry while outside the United States.

Federal permits are required by the U.S. Fish and Wildlife Service for the importation and exportation of most bird species listed under the Convention on International Trade in Endangered Species, endangered birds and native species, including feathers, parts and mounted specimens, and certain live injurious species. In addition, foreign wildlife permits may be required. Be sure to check with the foreign country for its wildlife requirements. U.S. Fish and Wildlife Service clearance is required to import and export all non-domestic birds and their parts and products.

Because certain States administer their own regulations to protect wildlife and animal health, you should contact appropriate State officials to learn about State requirements, if any, when making importation arrangements.

Cats

All domestic cats must be free of evidence of disease communicable to humans when examined at the port of entry. If the animal is not in apparent good health, further examination by a licensed veterinarian may be required at the owner's expense. Cats arriving in Hawaii or Guam, both of which are free of rabies, are subject to that state's/ territory's quarantine requirements.

Dogs

Domestic dogs must be free of evidence of diseases communicable to humans when examined at the port of entry. If the animal is not in apparent good health, further examination by a licensed veterinarian may be required at the owner's expense.

Dogs must be vaccinated against rabies at least 30 days before entering the United States. This requirement does not apply, however, to puppies less than three months of age or to dogs originating or located for at least six months in areas designated by the U.S. Public Health Service as being rabies-free.

The following procedures pertain to dogs arriving from areas that are not free of rabies:

A valid rabies vaccination certificate should accompany the animal. This certificate should be in English or be accompanied by a translation. It should identify the animal, the dates of vaccination and expiration, and be signed by a licensed veterinarian. If no expiration date is specified, the certificate is acceptable if the date of vaccination is no more than 12 months before the date of arrival.

If a vaccination has not been performed, or if the certificate is not valid, the animal may be admitted if it is confined immediately upon arrival at a place of the owner's choosing. The dog must be vaccinated within four days after arrival at the final destination, but no more than 10 days after arrival at the port of entry. The animal must remain in confinement for at least 30 days after being vaccinated.

If the vaccination was performed less than 30 days before arrival, the animal may be admitted but must be confined at a place of the owner's choosing until at least 30 days have passed since the vaccination.

Young puppies must be confined at a place of the owner's choosing until they are three months old, then they must be vaccinated. They must remain in confinement for 30 days.

Dogs that arrive in Hawaii or Guam, both of which are free of rabies, are subject to the state's or territory's quarantine requirements, in addition to whatever other Public Health Service requirements, above, apply.

Also be aware if you are going to be a dog owner in the United States, It is illegal not to clear up after your dog (You WILL be fined) Take a 'Poopa Scoopa' and a plastic bag with you. Dog excrement is called "Dog Doo" or "Doo Doo" in polite circles. You should also take out liability insurance. If your dog bites someone expect to be sued and for thousands.

Monkeys

Monkeys and other primates may be brought into the United States for scientific, educational or exhibition purposes by importers who are registered with the Centers for Disease Control and Prevention (CDC). However, under no circumstances may they be imported as pets. Registered importers who wish to import or export primates for a permitted purpose in accordance with CDC requirements are also required to obtain clearance from the U.S. Fish and Wildlife Service. The Convention on International Trade in Endangered Species (CITES) requires that all primates have permits.

Turtles

Live turtles with shells less than four inches long (linear measure) may not be imported for commercial purposes. An individual may import live turtles with shells less than four inches long and may also import viable turtle eggs, provided that for each arrival, there is no more than one lot containing fewer than seven viable turtle eggs, or any combination thereof totaling less than seven.

There are no Public Health Service restrictions on the importation of live turtles with a shell longer than four inches. Turtles are subject to all requirements of the U.S. Fish and Wildlife Service, which are outlined below.

Wildlife

The following categories of wildlife and fish are subject to certain prohibitions, restrictions, permits and quarantine requirements:

Mammals, birds, amphibians, fish, insects, crustaceans, mollusks, and other invertebrates.

Any part or products, such as feathers, skins, eggs; and articles manufactured from wildlife.

Federal laws prohibit the importation or transportation of any wildlife or wildlife parts that violate state or foreign laws.

The following ports are designated for entry of all fish and wildlife: Atlanta, Baltimore, Boston, Chicago, Dallas/Ft. Worth, Honolulu, Los Angeles, Miami, New Orleans, New York/Newark, Portland, San Francisco, and Seattle. All such packages and containers must be marked, labeled or tagged to plainly indicate the name and address of the shipper and consignee, and the number and nature of contents. Wildlife in any form, including pets, imported into or exported from the United States must be declared and cleared on U.S. Fish and Wildlife Form 3-177

(Declaration for Importation or Exportation of Fish or Wildlife) by the U.S. Fish and Wildlife Service prior to release by U.S. Customs. Contact the U.S. Fish and Wildlife Service for further clearance requirements and for a copy of the pamphlets Facts about Federal Wildlife Laws and Buyer Beware. Also contact the National Center for Import and Export of the Animal and Plant Health Inspection Service (contact information is listed at the bottom of this page) for information about importing animal and bird products such as hides, eggs, feathers, etc.

Endangered Species

The United States is a party in the Convention on International Trade in Endangered Species of Wild Fauna and Flora, commonly known as CITES. This treaty regulates trade in endangered species of wildlife, plants and their products. International trade in species listed by CITES is illegal unless authorized by permit. Items prohibited by CITES include, but are not limited to, articles made from whale teeth, ivory, tortoise shell, reptile, fur skins, coral, and birds. Permits to import into or export from the United States and re-export certificates are issued by the Office of Management Authority of the U.S. Fish and Wildlife Service (contact information is listed at the bottom of this page). Information on wildlife and plants, including lists of endangered species, may be obtained from that agency.

Before you contact any of the lists on the next few pages you should in the first instance contact your flight company. British Airways, Virgin Airways or whoever you are flying with. On the company's websites it has full details of how to bring an animal to the United States.

To learn clearance requirements for fish and wildlife:
U.S. Fish and Wildlife Service
Office of Law Enforcement
P.O. Box 3247
Arlington, Virginia 22203
http://www.fws.gov (Law Enforcement)

To obtain wildlife permits:
U.S. Fish and Wildlife Service
Office of Management Authority
4401 N. Fairfax Drive, Room 700
Arlington, Virginia 22203
Tel. 1-800-358-2104
Fax (703)358-2281
http://www.fws.gov (International Affairs)

U.S. Customs Service
Washington, DC 20229
Tel. (202) 927-6724
http://www.customs.gov

U.S. Public Health Service
Centers for Disease Control and Prevention
Division of Quarantine (E-03)
Atlanta, GA 30333
Tel. (404)639-8107
http://www.cdc.gov/ncidod/dq/animal.htm and
http://www.cdc.gov/od/ohs/biosfty/imprtper.htm

National Center for Import and Export
Animal and Plant Health Inspection Service
U.S. Department of Agriculture
Unit 40
Riverdale, MD 20737-1234
Tel. (301)734-3277
Fax (301)734-8226
http://www.aphis.usda.gov/ncie

Section 36) Weights and Measures.

Woman's Clothing

UK	8	10	12	14	16	18	20	22	24	26
USA	6	8	10	12	14	16	18	20	22	24
EU	34	36	38	40	42	44	46	48	50	52

Sweaters

	Woman's						Men's					
UK	34 36 38 40 42 44						34 36	38 40	42 44	46 48
USA	34 36 38 40 42 44						small	medium	large	X large

Children's Clothes

UK	16/18	20/22	24/26	28/30	32/34	36/38
USA	2	4	6	8	10	12

Shoes (Woman's and Mens)

Euro	35	35	36	37	37	38	39	39	40	40	41	42	42	43	44	44
UK	2	3	3	4	4	5	5	6	6	7	7	8	8	9	9	9
USA	4	4	5	5	6	6	7	7	8	8	9	9	10	10	11	11

Weight

Avoirdupois	Metric	Metric	Avoirdupois
1 oz	28.35g	1g	0.035 oz

Avoirdupois	Metric	Metric	Avoirdupois (cont)
1 pound*	454 g	100 g	3.5 oz
1 cwt	50.8 kg	250 g	9 oz
1 ton	1,016 kg	500 g	18 oz
1 tonne	2, 2025 pounds	1 kg	2.2 pounds

Capacity

Imperial	Metric	Metric	Imperial
1 pint (USA)	0.47 litre	1 litre	1.76 UK pints
1 pint (UK)	0.57 litre	1 litre	0.26 US gallons
1 gallon (USA)	3.78 litre	1 litre	0.22 UK gallon
1 gallon (UK)	4.54 litre	1 litre	35.21 Fluid oz

Temperature

Celsius	Fahrenheit	
0	32	(Freezing point of water)
5	41	
10	50	
15	59	
20	68	
25	77	

* A metric 'pound' is 500g, g = gramme, kg = kilograms

Celsius	Fahrenheit (cont)
30	86
35	95
40	104
50	122

(To convert Celsuis to Fahrenheit: multiply by 9, divide by 5 and add32. Fahrenheit to Celsius: subtract 32, multiply by 5 and divide by 9)

<u>Section 37)</u> Important Contact Information and Embassy Address Lists and Web Sites.

Below is a list of foreign embassy addresses. In addition to these addresses most states have consulates, you can find these via the internet or telephone directories.

Afghanistan Embassy of the Republic of Afghanistan
2341 Wyoming Avenue, NW
Washington, DC 20008

Algeria Embassy of the Democratic and Popular Republic of Algeria
2118 Kalorama Road, NW
Washington, DC 20008

Antigua and Barbuda Embassy of Antigua and Barbuda
2400 International Drive, NW, Suite 2H
Washington, DC 20008

Argentina Embassy of the Argentine Republic
1600 New Hampshire Avenue, NW
Washington, DC 20009 Tel (202) 238-6424
www.embassyofargentina-usa.org

Australia Embassy of Australia
1601 Massachusetts Avenue, NW
Washington, DC 20036 Telephone: (202) 797 3000

Austria Embassy of Austria

2343 Massachusetts Avenue, NW

Washington, DC 20008 Telephone (202) 895-6700

www.austrian-embassy.hu

Bahamas Embassy of the Commonwealth of the Bahamas

600 New Hampshire Avenue, NW, Suite 865

Washington, DC 20037

Bahrain Embassy of the State of Bahrain

3502 International Drive, NW

Washington, DC 20008

Bangladesh Embassy of the People's Republic of Bangladesh

2201 Wisconsin Avenue, NW

Washington, DC 20007

Barbados Embassy of Barbados

2144 Wyoming Avenue, NW

Washington, DC 20008

Belgium Embassy of Belgium

3330 Garfield Street, NW

Washington, DC 20008 (202) 333-6900 www.diplobel.us

Belize Embassy of Belize

3400 International Drive, NW, Suite 2J

Washington, DC 20008 (202) 332-9636

www.embassyofbelize.org

Benin Embassy of the People's Republic of Benin
2737 Cathedral Avenue, NW
Washington, DC 20008

Bolivia Embassy of Bolivia
3014 Massachusetts Avenue, NW
Washington, DC 20008

Botswana Embassy of the Republic of Botswana
4301 Connecticut Avenue, NW, Suite 404
Washington, DC 20008

Brazil Brazilian Embassy
3006 Massachusetts Avenue, NW
Washington, DC 20008 (202) 238-2700
www.brazilianembassy.org.il

Brunei Embassy of the State of Brunei DARUSSALAM
Watergate, Suite 300, 3rd Floor
2600 Virginia Avenue, NW
Washington, DC 20037 (202) 237-1838
www.bruneiembassy.org

Bulgaria Embassy of the People's Republic of Bulgaria
1621 22nd Street, NW
Washington, DC 20008 (202) 387-7969 www.bulgaria-embassy.org

Burkina Faso Embassy of Burkina Faso
2340 Massachusetts Avenue, NW
Washington, DC 20008

Burma (Myanmar) Embassy of the Union of Burma
2300 S Street, NW
Washington, DC 20008

Burundi Embassy of the Republic of Burundi
2233 Wisconsin Avenue, NW, Suite 212
Washington, DC 20007

Cameroon Embassy of the Republic of Cameroon
2349 Massachusetts Avenue, NW
Washington, DC 20008 (202) 265-8790 www.ambacam-usa.org

Canada Embassy of Canada
501 Pennsylvania Avenue, NW Washington, DC 20001 (202) 682-1740 www.canadaembassy.org Hours: 9 am to 4:30 pm, Monday to Friday Fax: (202) 682-7619

Cape Verde Embassy of the Republic of Cape Verde
3415 Massachusetts Avenue, NW
Washington, DC 20007

Central African Republic Embassy of Central African Republic
1618 22nd Street, NW
Washington, DC 20008

Chad Embassy of the Republic of Chad
2002 R Street, NW
Washington, DC 20009

Chile Embassy of Chile

1732 Massachusetts Avenue, NW

Washington, DC 20036 (202) 785-1746 www.chile-usa.org

China Embassy of the People's Republic of China

2300 Connecticut Avenue, NW

Washington, DC 20008 (202) 332-8851 www.china-embassy.org Fax: (202) 588-9760

Colombia Embassy of Colombia

2118 Leroy Pl., NW

Washington, DC 20008

Comoros Embassy of the Federal & Islamic Republic of the Comoros

C/o the Permanent Mission of the Federal &; Islamic Republic of the Comoros to the United States

336 East 45th Street, 2nd Floor

New York, NY 10017

Congo, People's Republic of: Embassy of the People's Republic of the Congo

4891 Colorado Avenue, NW

Washington, DC 20011

Costa Rica Embassy of Costa Rica

1825 Connecticut Avenue, NW, Suite 211

Washington, DC 20009 (202) 234-2945 www.costarica-embassy.org

Cote d'Ivoire (Ivory Coast) Embassy of the Republic of Cote d'Ivoire

2424 Massachusetts Avenue, NW

Washington, DC 20008

Cyprus Embassy of the Republic of Cyprus

2211 R Street, NW

Washington, DC 20008 (202) 462-5772
www.cyprusembassy.net

Czechoslovakia Embassy of the Czechoslovak Socialist Republic

3900 Linnean Avenue, NW

Washington, DC 20008

Cuban Interests Section Cuban Interests Section

2630 and 2639 16th Street, NW

Washington, DC 20009

Denmark Royal Danish Embassy

3200 Whitehaven Street, NW

Washington, DC 20008 (202) 234-4300
www.ambwashington.um.dk

Djibouti
Embassy of the Republic of Djibouti
866 United Nations Plaza
New York, NY 10011

Dominica Embassy of the Commonwealth of Dominica
205 Yoakum Pkwy, #823
Alexandria, VA 22304

Dominican Republic Embassy of the Dominican Republic
1715 22nd Street, NW
Washington, DC 20008

Ecuador Embassy of Ecuador
2535 15th Street, NW
Washington, DC 20009 (202) 234-7200

Embassy of the Arab Republic of Egypt
2310 Decatur Pl., NW
Washington, DC 20008

El Salvador Embassy of El Salvador
2308 California Street, NW
Washington, DC 20008 (202) 232-3763 (202) 265-9671

Equatorial Guinea Embassy of Equatorial Guinea
801 Second Avenue, Suite 1403
New York, NY 10017

Estonia Legation of Estonia
9 Rockefeller Plaza
New York, NY 10020

Ethiopia Embassy of Ethiopia
2134 Kalorama Road, NW
Washington, DC 20008 (202) 364-1200
www.ethiopianembassy.org

Fiji Embassy of Fiji
2233 Wisconsin Avenue, NW, Suite 240
Washington, DC 20007

Finland Embassy of Finland
3216 New Mexico Avenue, NW
Washington, DC 20016 (202) 298-5800

France Embassy of France
4101 Reservoir Road, NW
Washington, DC 20007 (202) 944-6000 www.ambafrance-us.org

Gabon Embassy of the Gabonese Republic
2034 20th Street, NW
Washington, DC 20009

The Gambia Embassy of the Gambia
19 East 42nd Street
New York, NY 10017

German Democratic Republic Embassy of the German Federal Republic
4645 Reservoir Road, NW
Washington, DC 20007

Ghana Embassy of Ghana
2460 16th Street, NW
Washington, DC 20009 (202) 686-4520 www.ghana-embassy.org

Greece Embassy of Greece
2221 Massachusetts Avenue, NW
Washington, DC 20008 (202) 332-8145

Grenada Embassy of Grenada

1701 New Hampshire Avenue, NW

Washington, DC 20009 Telephone: (202) 265-2561 Fax: (202) 265-2468

Guatemala Embassy of Guatemala

2220 R Street, NW

Washington, DC 20008 (202) 745-4952 www.guatemala-embassy.org

Guinea Embassy of the Republic of Guinea

2112 Leroy Pl., NW

Washington, DC 20008

Guinea-Bissau Embassy of the Republic of Guinea-Bissau

C/o Permanent Mission of Guinea- Bissau

211 E. 43rd Street, Suite 604

New York, NY 10017 202-947-3958

Guyana Embassy of Guyana

2490 Tracy Pl., NW

Washington, DC 20008 (202) 265-6900

Haiti Embassy of Haiti

2311 Massachusetts Avenue, NW

Washington, DC 20008

Holy See Apostolic Nunciature

3339 Massachusetts Avenue, NW

Washington, DC 20008

Honduras Embassy of Honduras
4301 Connecticut Avenue, NW,Suite 100
Washington, DC 20008 (202) 966-7702

Hungary Embassy of the Hungarian People's Republic
3910 Shoemaker Street, NW
Washington, DC 20008 (202) 362-6731

Iceland Embassy of Iceland
2022 Connecticut Avenue, NW
Washington, DC 20008

India Embassy of India
2107 Massachusetts Avenue, NW
Washington, DC 20008 202-9397000 Fax: 00-1-202-2654351
www.indianembassy.org

Indonesia Embassy of the Republic of Indonesia
2020 Massachusetts Avenue, NW
Washington, DC 20036

Iraq Embassy of the Republic of Iraq
1801 P Street, NW
Washington, DC 20036 (202) 483-7500
www.iraqiembassy.org

Ireland Embassy of Ireland
2234 Massachusetts Avenue, NW
Washington, DC 20008 (202) 462-3939 www.irelandemb.org

Israel Embassy of Israel
3514 International Drive, NW
Washington, DC 20008

Italy Embassy of Italy
1601 Fuller Street, NW
Washington, DC 20009 (202) 518-2139 www.italyemb.org

Jamaica Embassy of Jamaica
1850 K Street, NW, Suite 355
Washington, DC 20006 (202) 452-0660
www.jamaicaembassy.org

Japan Embassy of Japan
2520 Massachusetts Avenue, NW
Washington, DC 20008 Tel: 202-238-6700, Fax: 202-328-2187

Jordan Embassy of the Hashemite Kingdom of Jordan
3504 International Drive, NW
Washington, DC 20008 (202) 966-2664

Kenya Embassy of Kenya
2249 R Street, NW
Washington, DC 20008 (202) 387-6101

Korea, South Embassy of Korea
2320 Massachusetts Avenue, NW
Washington, DC 20008

Kuwait Embassy of the State of Kuwait
2940 Tilden Street, NW
Washington, DC 20008 Telephone: (202) 966-0702 Fax:
(202) 364-2868

Laos Embassy of the Lao People's Democratic Republic
2222 S Street, NW
Washington, DC 20008

Latvia Legation of Latvia
4325 17th Street, NW
Washington, DC 20011

Lebanon Embassy of Lebanon
2560 28th Street, NW
Washington, DC 20008 (202) 939-6300
www.lebanonembassyus.org

Lesotho Embassy of the Kingdom of Lesotho
2511 Massachusetts Avenue, NW
Washington, DC 20008

Liberia Embassy of the Republic of Liberia
5201 16th Street, NW
Washington, DC 20011 Tel: (202) 723-0437 Fax: (202) 723-
0436

Lithuania Legation of Lithuania
2622 16th Street, NW
Washington, DC 20009 (202) 234-5860

Luxembourg Embassy of Luxembourg
2200 Massachusetts Avenue, NW
Washington, DC 20008 (202) 265-4171 www.luxembourg-usa.org

Madagascar Embassy of the Democratic Republic of Madagascar
2374 Massachusetts Avenue, NW
Washington, DC 20008 (202) 265-5525 www.go2madagascar.net

Malawi: Malawi Embassy
2408 Massachusetts Avenue, NW
Washington, DC 20008 202 7971007

Malaysia Embassy of Malaysia
2401 Massachusetts Avenue, NW
Washington, DC 20008 (202) 572-9700

Mali Embassy of the Republic of Mali
2130 R Street, NW
Washington, DC 20008

Malta Embassy of Malta
2017 Connecticut Avenue, NW
Washington, DC 20008 (202) 462-3611

Mauritania Embassy of the Islamic Republic of Mauritania
2129 Leroy Pl., NW
Washington, DC 20008

Mauritius Embassy of Mauritius
4301 Connecticut Avenue, NW, Suite 134
Washington, DC 20008

Mexico Embassy of Mexico
2829 16th Street, NW
Washington, DC 20009 (202) 728-1628 Fax. (202) 234-4498

Mongolia Embassy of the Mongolian People's Republic
3636 16th Street, NW
Washington, DC 20010 (202) 333-7117

Morocco Embassy of Morocco
1601 21st Street, NW
Washington, DC 20009 (202) 457-0012

Mozambique Embassy of the People's Republic of
Mozambique
1990 M Street, NW, Suite 570
Washington, DC 20036 (202) 293-7146 www.embamoc-
usa.org

Nepal Royal Nepalese Embassy
2131 Leroy Pl., NW
Washington, DC 20000 (202) 667 4550
www.nepalembassyusa.org

Netherlands Embassy of the Netherlands
4200 Linnean Avenue, NW
Washington, DC 20008 (202) 244-5300

New Zealand Embassy of New Zealand

37 Observatory Circle, NW

Washington, DC 20008 (202) 328-4800

www.nzembassy.com

Nicaragua Embassy of Nicaragua

1627 New Hampshire Avenue, NW

Washington, DC 20009 (202) 939-6531

www.consuladodenicaragua.com

Niger Embassy of the Republic of Niger

2204 R Street, NW

Washington, DC 20008

Nigeria Embassy of the Federal Republic of Nigeria

2201 M Street, NW

Washington, DC 20037

Norway Royal Norwegian Embassy

2720 34th Street, NW

Washington, DC 20008 (202) 333-6000 www.norway.org

Oman Embassy of the Sultanate of Oman

2342 Massachusetts Avenue, NW

Washington, DC 20008

Pakistan Embassy of Pakistan

2315 Massachusetts Avenue, NW

Washington, DC 20008 (202) 939-6202

Panama Embassy of Panama

2862 McGill Terrace, NW

Washington, DC 20008 (202) 965-4819

www.embassyofpanama.org

Papua New Guinea Embassy of Papua New Guinea

1330 Connecticut Avenue, NW, Suite 350

Washington, DC 20036

Paraguay Embassy of Paraguay

2400 Massachusetts Avenue, NW

Washington, DC 20008 (202) 483-6960

Peru Embassy of Peru

1700 Massachusetts Avenue, NW

Washington, DC 20036 (202) 833-9860 (202) 462-1084 (202) 363-4808

Philippines Embassy of the Philippines

1617 Massachusetts Avenue, NW

Washington, DC 20036 (202) 467-9300

www.philippineembassy-usa.org

Poland Embassy of the Polish People's Republic

2640 16th Street, NW

Washington, DC 20009 phone: (202) 234-3800 fax: (202) 328-2152 www.polandembassy.org

Portugal Embassy of Portugal

2125 Kalorama Road, NW

Washington, DC 20008 (202) 328-8610

Qatar Embassy of the State of Qatar
Suite 1180
600 New Hampshire Avenue, NW
Washington, DC 20037

Romania Embassy of the Socialist Republic of Romania
1607 23rd Street, NW
Washington, DC 20008 (202) 232-4747 www.roembus.org

Rwanda Embassy of the Republic of Rwanda
1714 New Hampshire Avenue, NW
Washington, DC 20009

Saint Kitts and Nevis Embassy of St. Kitts and Nevis
2501 M Street, NW, Suite 540
Washington, DC 20037

Saint Lucia Embassy of Saint Lucia
2100 M Street, NW, Suite 309
Washington, DC 20037

Sao Tome and Principe Embassy of Sao Tome and Principe
801 Second Avenue, Suite 1504
New York, NY 10017

Saudi Arabia Embassy of Saudi Arabia
601 New Hampshire Avenue, NW
Washington, DC 20037

Senegal Embassy of the Republic of Senegal
2112 Wyoming Avenue, NW
Washington, DC 20008

Seychelles Embassy of the Republic of Seychelles
C/o Permanent Mission of Seychelles to the United Nations
820 Second Avenue, Suite 927
New York, NY 10017

Sierra Leone Embassy of Sierra Leone
1701 19th Street, NW
Washington, DC 20009

Singapore Embassy of Singapore
1824 R Street, NW
Washington, DC 20009 (202) 537-3100 www.mfa.gov.sg

Somalia Embassy of the Somali Democratic Republic
600 New Hampshire Avenue, NW, Suite 710
Washington, DC 20037

South Africa Embassy of South Africa
3051 Massachusetts Avenue, NW
Washington, DC 20008

Spain Embassy of Spain
2700 15th Street, NW
Washington, DC 20009 (202) 452 0100

Sri Lanka Embassy of the Democratic Socialist Republic of Sri
Lanka
2148 Wyoming Avenue, NW
Washington, DC 20008

Sudan Embassy of the Republic of the Sudan
2210 Massachusetts Avenue, NW
Washington, DC 20008

Suriname Embassy of the Republic of Suriname
2600 Virginia Avenue, NW
Washington, DC 20037

Swaziland Embassy of the Kingdom of Swaziland
4301 Connecticut Avenue, NW
Washington, DC 20008

Sweden Embassy of Sweden
600 New Hampshire Avenue, NW, Suite 1200
Washington, DC 20037 Tel: (202) 467-2600
www.swedenabroad.com

Switzerland Embassy of Switzerland
2900 Cathedral Avenue, NW
Washington, DC 20008 Tel. +1 202 745 7900 Fax +1 202 387
2564 www.swissemb.org
Monday-Thursday 8:00-17:00 Friday 8:00-16:00

Syria Embassy of the Syrian Arab Republic
2215 Wyoming Avenue, NW
Washington, DC 20008 (202) 232-6313
www.syriaembassy.org

Tanzania Embassy of the United Republic of Tanzania
2139 R Street, NW
Washington, DC 20008 (202) 939-6125
www.tanzaniaembassy-us.org

Thailand Embassy of Thailand
2300 Kalorama Road, NW
Washington, DC 20008 (202) 467-6790

Togo Embassy of the Republic of Togo
2208 Massachusetts Avenue, NW
Washington, DC 20008 (202) 234-4212

Trinidad and Tobago Embassy of Trinidad and Tobago
1708 Massachusetts Avenue, NW
Washington, DC 20036 (202) 467-6490 www.trinidad-and-tobago.com

Tunisia Embassy of Tunisia
1515 Massachusetts Avenue, NW
Washington, DC 20005 (202) 862-1850

Turkey Embassy of the Republic of Turkey
1606 23rd Street, NW
Washington, DC 20008 (202) 612-6712
www.turkishembassy.org

Uganda Embassy of the Republic of Uganda
5909 16th Street, NW
Washington, DC 20011 (202) 726-7100
www.ugandaembassy.com

Union of Soviet Socialist Republics Embassy of the Union of
Soviet Socialist Republics
1125 16th Street, NW
Washington, DC 20036

United Arab Emirates Embassy of the United Arab Emirates
600 New Hampshire Avenue, NW, Suite 740
Washington, DC 20037

United Kingdom of Great Britain and Northern Ireland
British Embassy
3100 Massachusetts Avenue, NW
Washington, DC 20008 (202) 588-7800 (202) 588-6500
(202) 331-8947 www.bdsw.org www.britain-info.org

Uruguay Embassy of Uruguay
1919 F Street, NW
Washington, DC 20006 (202) 331-1313 www.uruwashi.org

Venezuela Embassy of Venezuela
2445 Massachusetts Avenue, NW
Washington, DC 20008 (202) 234-0225 www.embavenez-us.org

Western Samoa Embassy of Western Samoa
C/o Permanent Mission of Samoa to the United Nations
820 2nd Avenue
New York, NY 10017

Yemen Embassy of the Yemen Arab Republic
600 New Hampshire Avenue, NW, Suite 840
Washington, DC 20037 (202) 965-4760
www.yemenembassy.org

Yugoslavia Embassy of the Socialist Federal Republic of
Yugoslavia
2410 California Street, NW
Washington, DC 20008 (202) 332-9044,

Zaire Embassy of the Republic of Zaire
1800 New Hampshire Avenue, NW
Washington, DC 20009 (202) 234 7690

Zambia Embassy of the Republic of Zambia
2419 Massachusetts Avenue, NW
Washington, DC 20008 (202) 265-9717
www.zambiaembassy.org

Zimbabwe Embassy of Zimbabwe
2852 McGill Terrace, NW
Washington, DC 20008 (202) 332-3628 www.zimbabwe-embassy.us

Delegation of the Commission of the European Communities
2100 M. Street, NW, 7th Floor
Washington, DC 20037

Marshall Islands
Representative Office of the of Republic of the Marshall Islands
1901 Pennsylvania Avenue, NW, Suite 1004
Washington, DC 20006

Micronesia
Representative Office of the Federated States of Micronesia
706 G Street, SE
Washington, DC 20003

Useful Websites

Links to most embassy internet sites can be found at www.info.gov.

Gun control and Law: www.gunlaws.com

Auto Prices: www.kellysbluebook.com

Brits overseas: www.homesoverseas.co.uk
www.britsinamerica.com www.sunnybrits.com
www.british-expats.com www.thebrits.com
www.britsonline.com www.floridabritishclub.com
www.britishbureau.com www.backinblighty.com
www.britishinamerica.com

Real-estate and property search: www.realtor.com

www.ins.usdoj.gov/graphics/aboutins/statistics
Immigration & Naturalization Service (INS) site
Information about foreign nationals who enter or attempt
to enter for permanent residence. Also gives subsequent
actions – apprehensions, removal, and naturalization.
Periodic reports published. Links to U.S. Dept. of Justice
sites.

www.census.gov/population/socdemo/foreign
U.S. Census Bureau site
Current Population Survey (CPS) - data on characteristics of
native- and foreign-born population. Includes legal
immigrants, undocumented immigrants, temporary
residents (students, workers on business visas).www.irsa-
uscr.org

IRSA: Immigration and Refugee Services of America
Located in Washington, D.C. Helps refugees become
oriented in U.S.; gives information on how to help refugees.

www.ins.usdoj.gov/graphics/index.htm
Immigration and Naturalization Service
Answers frequently-asked questions about procedures at
INS. Includes forms. Historical immigration facts and
numbers. Agency oversees citizenship, asylum, permanent
residency, refugee status, inter-country adoption, family,
employment, and student authorization. Various links for
recent changes in border rulings for Mexico and Canada.

www.usdoj.gov/eoir
Dept. of Justice, Executive Office for Immigration Review site
with Board of Immigration Appeals from Oct. 1996 - date.
Sets standards, implements process in criminal alien cases.

www.usdoj.gov/crt/osc
Dept. of Justice, Office of Special Counsel for Immigration-
Related Unfair Employment Practices
Site has fact sheets, forms, brochures and press releases. In
English or Spanish.

FAIR: The Federation for American Immigration Reform
Located in Washington, D.C. Includes population figures,
immigration figures, projections, legislation and updates,
related issues. Links to legislation and Congressional
members.

www.immigration-usa.com
Commercial software company sells Immigration
Assistant/Personal edition for individuals; Immigration USA
for legal professionals.

www.usa-green-card.com
Gives application and requirement information for the
Green Card lottery. Available in German, Spanish, French,
Italian and Portuguese.

American School Directory www.asd.com

American Teachers Abroad www.overseasdigest.com

Life in America General info for immigrants www.lifeinthe usa.com

General Travel information Visit USA www.visitusa.org.uk

Expatriate Mothers www.expatmoms.com

Please note, *The Author and the publishers do not endorse, recommend or have any input on the websites and phone numbers given. They are here for your reference, with a view to seeking general information about America and Immigration .You search these websites and use the information at your own risk.*

Phone numbers: United States

Immigration and Naturalization Service (General):
1-800-375-5283

INS Forms (to order by Phone):
1-800-870-3676

INS National Customer Service Information:
1-800-375-5283

INS Texas Service Center:
Phone: 214-381-1423

INS Nebraska Service Center:
Phone: 402-323-7830

INS California Service Center:
Phone: 949-831-8427

INS Vermont Service Center:
Phone: 802-527-4913

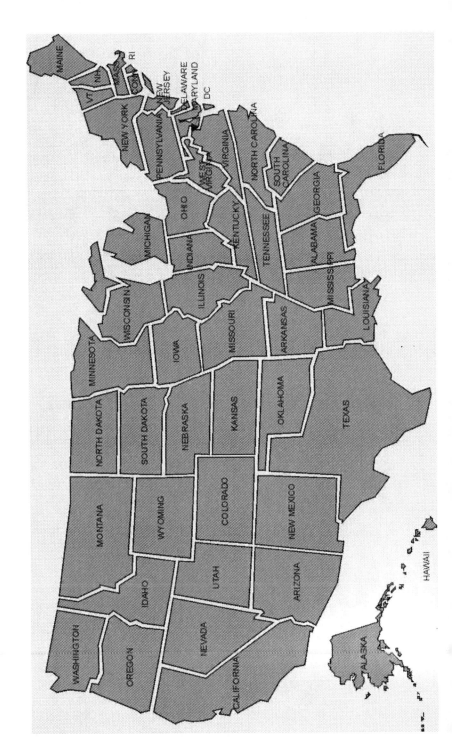

Photographic Credits.

Most images and all cartoons by the author, some from Public domain and

Geographical Magazine

Flex Magazine

Cigar Aficionado Magazine

Sports Weekly Memphis

UK. The Sunday Times Supplement.

Section 38) Glossary of Buying a Home in America.

Acceleration clause: A clause in your mortgage which allows the lender to demand payment of the loan balance for various reasons.

Acceptance: Agreeing to accept an offer on a property, which constitutes a contract.

Adjustable rate Mortgage (ARM): A type of mortgage in which the interest changes periodically up or down, according to corresponding fluctuations in an index. All ARMS are tied to indexes. Available nationwide, also called 'A variable rate mortgage'

Ad Valorem Tax: A tax based on the value of the property. I.e. property or real estate taxes.

Adjustment Date: The date the interest rate changes on an adjustable rate mortgage.

Amortization: The gradual process of systematically reducing debt in equal payments (As in a mortgage) comprising both principal and interest, until the debt is paid in full.

Amortization Schedule: A table which shows how much of each payment will be applied towards principal and how much toward interest over the life of the loan. It can also show the gradual decrease of the balance until it reaches zero.

Annual Percentage rate (APR): It not actually the interest rate on your loan/mortgage. APR measures the net effective cost of borrowing -- "the actual present value of those funds over the length of the contract." In other words, APR answers the question: "Is it worth it to pay more upfront to get a lower rate?" The APR is really the true cost of borrowing, expressed as a percentage. Deduct the closing costs from your loan amount, then using your actual loan payment; calculate what the interest rate would be on this amount instead of your actual loan amount. You will come up with a number close to the APR. Because you are using the same payment on a smaller amount, the APR is always higher than the actual note rate on your loan. Therefore INSIST on asking what the APR is before you sign anything. This way you can see a like for like loan.

Application: The form used to apply for a mortgage containing information about a borrower's income, savings, assets, debts and other details.

Appraisal: The professional examination of a property to determine its market value. This is done by a local licenses appraiser.

Appraised Value: An opinion of a property's fair market value based on an appraisers knowledge, experience and analysis of the property and sold prices properties of similar size in the same area. The appraisal usually comes out at the purchased priced.

Assessed Value: The value placed on a property for tax purposes by the county property appraiser.

Assignment: When ownership of your mortgage is transferred from one company or individual to another, it is called an assignment.

Assumable Mortgage: A loan which the bank/lender is willing to transfer from the current owner of a property to a new owner, normally at the same terms of interest rate and dates. This can be an advantage when you are trying to sell your home. However the new buyer must 'qualify' for the loan.

Assumption: The term applied when a buyer assumes the seller' mortgage.

Balloon Mortgage: balloon mortgage can be an excellent option for many home buyers. A balloon mortgage is usually rather short, with a term of five to seven years, but the payment is based on a term of 30 years. They often have a lower interest rate, and can be easier to qualify for than a traditional 30 year fixed mortgage. There is, however, a risk to consider. At the end of your loan term you will need to pay off your outstanding balance. This usually means you must refinance, sell your home or convert the balloon mortgage to a traditional mortgage at the current interest rates. The number of years over which you will repay this loan. The most common balloon mortgage terms are 5 years and 7 years. After the mortgage term is complete, you will then need to refinance or pay off the remaining balance.

Bankruptcy: The federal court proceeding by which a debtor (individual or corporation) may obtain protection from creditors. The two general types of bankruptcy are voluntary and involuntary. A voluntary bankruptcy is initiated when the debtor voluntarily files a petition. In an involuntary bankruptcy, the creditor forces the debtor into bankruptcy. Debtors qualifying as farmers may not be involuntarily forced into bankruptcy. Bankruptcy proceedings involving farmers are declared under one of the several chapters of the federal bankruptcy code: Chapter 7 - liquidation; Chapters 11 and 12 - reorganizations; Chapter 13 - adjustment and workouts of debt.

Bill of Sale: is a legal document made by a 'seller' to a *purchaser*, reporting that on a specific date, at a specific locality, and for a particular sum of money or other "value received", the seller sold to the purchaser a specific item of personal, or parcel of real, property of which he had lawful possession.

Bi-Weekly Mortgage: a biweekly mortgage can save you thousands of dollars. And that a biweekly mortgage can shave years off the life of your loan and help you accrue equity in your home fast. Instead of making one single monthly mortgage payment each month, or 12 mortgage payments a year, you make a mortgage payment every two weeks. And because there are 52 weeks in a year, that equates to 26 mortgage payments a year, or 13 total monthly payments. The result is an additional mortgage payment each year, but of course it's not that simple. Nothing ever is. You can't simply expect the bank or lender to allow you to mail in a half payment twice a month, which simply won't fly.

Cap rate Mortgage: The condition in a capped rate mortgage that sets a maximum interest rate for a specified period. See capped rate.

Cap and Collar Mortgage: A cap is a maximum rate of interest that can be charged for a specified period, while a collar is a minimum rate of interest that can be charged for a specified period.

Capped Rate: A capped rate mortgage sets a maximum rate of interest that the lender can charge, but only for a specified period.

Cash Back: An amount of money paid to the borrower by the lender at the end of a mortgage. A 'Cash Back mortgage' is one in which an amount of money is paid by the lender to the borrower at the start of the mortgage, typically to help with the costs of moving home.

Cash Back Remortgage: A remortgage that is structured so that the borrower receives a sum of money at the start of the new term. Also known as **Cash-Out finance.**

Clear Title: A legal term that refers to the clear ownership of a property. Also known as free and clear.

Collateral: An asset, such as a car or a home, which is used to guarantee the repayment of a loan. Should the borrower fail to repay the loan under the terms of the original contract, the asset may be seized by the lender.

Common Areas: Sections of land or buildings, such as gardens, hallways, recreational facilities and parking areas, where more than one resident shares access.

Completion & Closing: The completion date is the date on which your solicitor forwards the money from your lender to the solicitor of the vendor. It is the date that you become the legal owner of your new property.

Compound Interest: An interest payment on both capital and on previously accrued interest. For example, $100 borrowed for 5 years at 5% p.a. would become $105 after 1 year, S110.25 after 2 years, $115.76 after 3 years, and so on.

Closing Costs: Closing costs are separated into what are called 'non-recurring closing costs' and 'pre-paid items' Non-recurring closing closings are any items which are paid just once as a result of buying the property or obtaining the loan. A lender will make an attempt to estimate the amount of non-recurring closing costs and pre-paid items on the 'Good Faith Estimate' which they MUST issue to the borrower within 3 days of receiving the completed home loan application.

Condominium (Condo): A building or development that comprises of two or more units (sometimes 100's) the interior is individually owned. The walls, roof and common areas are jointly owned by all the unit owners.

Deed: The legal document conveying title to a property.

Delinquency: Failure to make mortgage payments on the due dates.

Easement: The interest, privilege or right of that a person has on the land of another person or party, example utility lines.

Encumbrance: Anything that affects or limits the fee simple title to a property, such as mortgages, leases, easements or restrictions.

Escrow: A procedure in which documents, although normally funds are put in the care of a third party, other than the buyer or seller, pending completion of agreed conditions and terms in sales contracts. An escrow company performs escrow services. You will use this method if you apply for an E-2 Visa. Your funds must be at risk.

Fixed rate Mortgage: A mortgage that has its interest rate set at an agreed percentage point.

Foreclosures. The legal process by which a borrower in default under a mortgage is deprived of his interest in the mortgaged property. This usually involves a forced sale of the property at public auction with the proceeds of the sale being applied to the mortgage debt. Foreclosure rates are high among ARM borrowers. ARM or adjustable rate mortgages frequently offer a low introductory interest rate, which is very tempting to potential homebuyers. Once signed on homeowners might experience an increase in their monthly payments due to increases in current interest rates. This might sometimes prove mortgage unaffordable to some homebuyers and lead to the loss of their property in a foreclosure.

FSBO: You will see these signs in America, it simply means for sale by owner. An owner will try and sell his home without a realtor and save fees. However they don't sell very fast and don't always get a good price.

Hazard Insurance: Insurance coverage that in the event of physical damage to a property from fire, wind, vandalism or other hazards.

Home Inspection: It is recommended that you hire a professional to perform a home inspection on the house you are interested in purchasing. A home inspection is an objective examination of the physical structure and systems of a home. Make sure the professional you hire inspects all the major systems in the house, such as heating and cooling, plumbing, and electrical.

If problems are identified, it doesn't necessarily mean you shouldn't buy the house. However, you should be aware of potential repairs. A seller may adjust the purchase price or contract terms if major problems are found. Or, you may decide not to purchase the home. You can make a purchase contingent on a satisfactory home inspection. Your realtor will recommend you have this done.

Home insurance: In the United States, most home buyers borrow money in the form of a mortgage loan, and the mortgage lender always requires that the buyer purchase homeowners insurance as a condition of the loan, in order to protect the bank if the home were to be destroyed. Anyone with an insurable interest in the property should be listed on the policy. In some cases the 'mortgagee' will waive the need for the mortgagor to carry homeowner's insurance if the value of the land exceeds the amount of the mortgage balance. In a case like this even the total destruction of any buildings would not affect the ability of the lender to be able to foreclose and recover the full amount of the loan. Key West Bank is one such bank that will waive windstorm insurance when the land value is higher than the loan amount.

The insurance crisis in Florida has meant that some waterfront property owners in that state have had to make that decision due to the high cost of premiums.

HUD: The US Department of housing and Urban Development (HUD), which sells homes deeded to HUD/FHA by mortgage companies who have been forced to foreclose on FHA-insured mortgages.

Hud-1 Settlement Statement: A document that provides an itemized listing of the funds that were paid at the closing. Items that can appear on a HUD statement include real estate commissions, loan fees, and initial escrow amounts. Each type of expense goes on the sheet. The Hud -1 statement is also known as the 'Closing statement' or settlement statement'.

Leasehold Estate: A way of holding title to a property wherein the mortgagor does not actually own the property but rather has a record of long term lease. These terms can range from 5 years to 999 years.

Lien: A legal claim against a property that must be paid off when the property is sold. A mortgage is also considered a lien.

Lot: The plots are parcel of land on which a home is built or even the land on which a mobile home is located.

Mortgage: A written instrument that creates a lien against real estate as security for the repayment of a loan.

a) Blanket mortgage - A lien on more than one parcel of real estate.

b) First mortgage - A real estate mortgage that has priority over all other mortgages on a specified piece of real estate.

c) Graduated payment mortgage - A type of delayed payment mortgage where the payments increase over time.

d) Second mortgage - The use of two lenders in a real estate mortgage in which one lender holds a first mortgage on the real estate and another lender holds a second mortgage. The first mortgage holder has first claim on the borrower's mortgaged property and assets in the event of loan default and foreclosure or bankruptcy.

e) Shared appreciation mortgage - A financing arrangement for real estate in which the lender reduces the interest rate on the loan in return for a stipulated share of the appreciated value of the land being financed at a designated time in the future. The risk of land value appreciation is shared between lender and borrower, and the lender's compensation from value appreciation generally occurs through refinancing in which the loan balance is increased by the amount of the shared appreciation.

Mortgage Insurance Premium: (MIP) This is an insurance plan or a charge paid by the borrower to obtain finance. This is normally a requirement when you less than 20% deposit. Please note: If you feel your property value has increased or you have repaid some of you're off to a level that gives you at least 30% equity, you can contact the lender and insist that they remove the MIP. You may have to pay the cost of an appraisal in most cases.

Multiple Listing Service: MLS as it is known. This is the broker information net work for Realtor's to list homes for sale or rent. Most homes for sale are advertised this way. You can get to the MLS by visiting a Realtor's website and following the links. Some Realtor's site will require you to register, if you do this expect to get a monthly or weekly news letter via e-mail and probably a follow up phone call.

Point: a point is 1% of the amount of the loan/mortgage.

Principal: The amount borrowed or remaining unpaid. The part of the monthly payment that reduces the remaining balance of a mortgage.

Principal and Interest Payment (P&I): A periodic (Monthly) mortgage payment that includes interest charges plus an amount applied to the amortization of the principle balance. Also known as a 'Re-payment loan/mortgage)

Promissory note: A written promise to pay a specified amount over a given time period.

Purchase Agreement: A written contract signed by the buyer and the seller stating the terms and conditions under which the property will be sold.

Refinancing: A change in an existing loan designed to extend and/or restructure the repayment obligation or to achieve more favorable loan terms by transferring the financing arrangement to another lender or loan type.

Risk Rating: The relative amount of credit risk associated with a loan transaction. The lender may use credit scoring or risk assessment procedures to evaluate loan requests and group borrowers into various risk classes for purposes of loan acceptance or rejection, loan pricing, loan control, degree of monitoring and level of loan documentation

Quitclaim deed: A deed that transfers without warranty whatever interest or title a grantor may have at the time the conveyance is made.

Title: The right of possession and legal evidence of ownership.

Title Insurance: Protects lenders and homeowners against loss of their interest in a property due to legal defects in title.

Title Search: A check of the title records to ensure that the seller is the legal owner of the property and that there are no liens or other claims outstanding.

Transfer of Ownership: Any means by which the ownership of a property changes hands.

Truth in Lending: The federal Truth in Lending Act is intended to assure a meaningful disclosure of credit terms to borrowers, especially on consumer loans. Lenders are required to inform borrowers precisely and explicitly of the total amount of the finance charge which they must pay and the annual percentage interest rate to the nearest .01%. Excluded transactions include loans for commercial or business purposes, including agricultural loans; loans to partnerships, corporation, cooperatives and organization; and loans greater than $25,000 except for owner-occupied, residential real estate mortgages where compliance is required regardless of the amount.

Variable Rate Mortgage (VRM): *See Adjustable Rate Mortgage.* A mortgage for which the rate of interest fluctuates as money market rates change. The payment will usually remain the same for the term. If rates increase to a point where the payment does not cover the interest, an increased payment or a pay down of the principal would be required

Zoning: Zoning is the way the governments control the physical development of land and the kinds of uses to which each individual property may be put. Zoning laws typically specify the areas in which residential, industrial, recreational or commercial activities may take place. For example, an R-1 residential zone might allow only single-family detached homes as opposed to duplexes or apartment complexes. On the other hand, a C-1 commercial zone might be zoned to permit only certain commercial or industrial uses in one jurisdiction, but permit a mix of housing and businesses in another jurisdiction.

Circa 2008

A Final Word from the Author.

For decades the United States of America has been recognized throughout the world as the "Land of Opportunity", making the goal of reaching its friendly shores the dream of millions of immigrants searching for a better life.

Give me your tired, your hungry, your poor, your oppressed, your weary...this is what the Statue of Liberty says to those who migrate across the ocean to America. Immigrants have heard the cries promising freedom, and a better life for centuries now. Hundreds of thousands, of people from around the world, have answered the call. Several songwriters have penned songs about America being the land of the free and a land filled with prosperity. Foreign lands and nations regard America as a proud country.

America has stood against and defeated many a foe. She is a country that stands up against injustice, others being treated inhumanely, and will fight to protect the rights of those who cannot fight for themselves. You are joining the many people from all around the world boldly leave their native country to make a living in the United States. These risk-takers total more than 1 million each year. The freedoms and opportunities offered to the people of the United States mean that whatever you can dare to dream and are willing to sacrifice to achieve, you can do. There will always be set-backs and failures, nay-sayers and skeptics...but the destiny of every United States citizen lies in their own willingness to dream and work to achieve those dreams. The truth of this fact is quickly evident in the Land of Opportunity room. Here you will meet the unlikeliest of heroes...men and women, boys and girls who faced challenges and obstacles that seemed insurmountable, yet went on to achieve beyond imagination. 80 percent live above the poverty line, and 69 percent of those who have lived here for 30 years or more own their own homes. Their culture of hard work, in other words, has enabled them to climb out of poverty, and they are going through the same powerful process of change as any of the immigrant groups that have come to the United States, melting gradually but inexorably into our middle and working classes.

Mark A Cooper *circa 2008*

With so much misinformation it is important you know what the visa requirements are and what visa is suitable for you and your family. The objective of this book is to provide a solid foundation to achieve personal and business success with your move to the United States. Whether it is a temporary or permanent move. I hope this will be just a part of the information you gain towards achievement of your vision and goals by instilling belief and commitment to free enterprise principles. Let me be the first to say, "Welcome to America".